WITHDRAWN

WIFE BEATER SHIRT
OPTIONAL

There is no dress code for domestic violence

Laura Streyffeler, Ph.D., LMHC

BALBOA
PRESS

A DIVISION OF HAY HOUSE

Balboa Press books may be ordered through booksellers or by contacting:

Balboa Press
A Division of Hay House
1663 Liberty Drive
Bloomington, IN 47403
www.balboapress.com
1 (877) 407-4847

Because of the dynamic nature of the Internet, any web addresses or links contained in this book may have changed since publication and may no longer be valid. The views expressed in this work are solely those of the author and do not necessarily reflect the views of the publisher, and the publisher hereby disclaims any responsibility for them.

The author of this book does not dispense medical advice or prescribe the use of any technique as a form of treatment for physical, emotional, or medical problems without the advice of a physician, either directly or indirectly. The intent of the author is only to offer information of a general nature to help you in your quest for emotional and spiritual well-being. In the event you use any of the information in this book for yourself, which is your constitutional right, the author and the publisher assume no responsibility for your actions.

Any people depicted in stock imagery provided by Thinkstock are models, and such images are being used for illustrative purposes only. Certain stock imagery © Thinkstock.

Print information available on the last page.

ISBN: 978-1-5043-8821-4 (sc)
ISBN: 978-1-5043-8823-8 (hc)
ISBN: 978-1-5043-8822-1 (e)

Library of Congress Control Number: 2017914730

Balboa Press rev. date: 10/17/2017

To every person who has trusted me enough to share their story, secrets, and soul with me, you have been my teacher. I honor you, I thank you, and I dedicate this book to you.

CONTENTS

PREFACE

M any years back, I was working with an upper-middle-class woman who came to see me because she was having, as she put it, "trouble in her marriage." She explained to me that her husband was jealous and controlling, called her names, treated her like his personal servant, and isolated her from her family and friends. She added that he "only hit me once, and that was because I wouldn't stop arguing and pushed him too far. It was my fault."

I explained to her that his inappropriate behavior was abusive and not her fault and that she was a victim of domestic violence. She responded, "That's not possible!" I asked her why she didn't believe that she was a victim of domestic violence. I was surprised by her response, in which she referred to women whom she considered actual victims of domestic violence: "You know, they live in trailer parks and their husbands wear "wifebeater shirts." Smiling at her naïveté, I said, "I didn't know there was a dress code for domestic violence!"

I later realized that her response was genuine. Due to a lack of information about domestic violence, she truly believed the myths perpetuated by bad television shows and popular culture. Since then, I have worked with a number of men and women who did not realize that the trouble in their relationship was abuse related. In twenty-five years of providing therapy to clients who report relationship problems, I have found many did not know that they were in abusive relationships. Even without the presence of physical violence, emotional and mental violence *are still violence.* They are being victimized, regardless of how strong, independent, intelligent, and/or financially secure they are! They are the catalysts that motivated me to write this book.

This Book Is Not for Victims Alone!

The more we understand about domestic violence, the better equipped we are to recognize and fight it.

In 1987, I moved to Florida with two suitcases and a $175.00 check in my wallet. I moved into my parents' garage apartment. I left everything else behind, including an abusive relationship. As part of my personal journey, filled with passion and a need for healing, I began volunteering at the local domestic and sexual violence shelter. Upon completion of my volunteer training, the shelter needed staff members; I became a residential crisis counselor and an on-call advocate to the hospitals and rape trauma center for victims of domestic and sexual violence. While working as a counselor, I began my masters in mental health counseling.

In June 1995, I started working at the local mental health counseling center, doing in home family counseling in cases of child abuse and neglect. Also, as part of my master's program, I interned with the local substance abuse treatment facility. During this internship, I developed and facilitated a program for teenagers arrested for domestic violence and their families. I ran and directed the program until 2001. I received my master's degree in 1996 and became a licensed mental health counselor in 1998. In 2001, I came full circle and returned to the domestic and sexual violence center as the clinical director and remained there for ten years, while also maintaining a part-time private practice.

In 2002, I started my PhD program and wrote my dissertation on the topic of traumatic stress in victims of domestic violence. In 2008, I published a research study that examined how licensed clinical professionals assess, diagnose, and treat victims of domestic violence. I learned that for many licensed clinical professionals, their knowledge of domestic violence, beyond the two-hour training required for licensure renewal, was often minimal. As a result, victims of domestic violence were being misdiagnosed and given inappropriate medication.

As a board-certified expert in traumatic stress and a clinically certified expert in domestic violence and forensic counseling, I have taught domestic violence courses at Florida Gulf Coast University to bachelor's level criminal justice students. In addition, I created and facilitated a master's level mental health counseling course in trauma at Hodges University. I've served as president of the county homeless coalition, spent eight years on a domestic violence fatality review board, was involved in the human trafficking task force, and have provided training to local agencies and community members. I have also taught domestic and sexual violence classes to both male and female inmates.

I wrote this book with the hope of educating and empowering all of those men and women who are, or have been, in controlling, abusive relationships and do not know it. By sharing some hypothetical examples, along with explanations and discussion, it is my hope that readers will see themselves in these scenarios, say "that happened to me" or "that is happening to me," and realize that they are in an abusive or controlling relationship, whether the relationship includes physical violence or not. More importantly, I hope readers realize that it is the relationship that is unhealthy, that they are not "crazy" or alone, and that they need to seek out professional help. If some of the stories seem similar or redundant, that is because domestic violence is a pattern of behavior, not a single act. The pattern and its related behaviors are often textbook cases, and although the victim feels at fault and alone, she or he often has more in common with other victims than one might think.

One quick note: men's white tank top undershirts are often referred to as *wifebeaters*, not *spouse beaters*, but perpetrators can be and often are females.

INTRODUCTION

I was working in a domestic violence shelter in the early 1990s, which included working a domestic violence hotline, before and during the O. J. Simpson trial. Back then, nobody talked about domestic violence. It was thought of as a family matter and never to be discussed in public. Airing your dirty laundry in public was against most family rules and appropriate social mores. As a result, people underestimated how many woman and men were being emotionally, mentally, physically, and/or sexually abused, manipulated, controlled, and/or threatened by their partners. Many of those who were being abused felt isolated, alone, and all too often, to blame.

At the time of the trial, no one wanted to believe that the beloved sports superstar, "The Juice," was capable of domestic violence or murder. His public image was that of a man who could do it all, had it all, and was loved and respected by all. He was a role model for America's youth. The O. J. Simpson trial began to open awareness and the conversation about domestic violence. Still, for many people, domestic violence was thought of as a physical violation, not an emotional, psychological or even a sexual one.

At the time this book is being written, domestic violence is still often thought to be more about physical violence than emotional or psychological abuse. Outsiders often blame the victim for his or her situation, saying, "I would never let a (wo)man treat me like that. If anyone ever hit me, I would just leave." Outsiders often don't know or care that victims are beaten down long before they are ever beaten up. In addition, domestic violence is about one partner having control over the other. Victims often fear the consequences of leaving, which means taking the control back or away from the controlling and/or abusive partner. Doing so, they fear, will escalate the situation rather than relieve it.

The word *victim* has so much judgment and stigma attached. As a result, there is a lack of awareness, a minimization, and/or a sense of denial about what domestic violence truly is—especially when there is no physical violence. No one wants to be or think of himself or herself as powerless or as a victim. Nor does anyone want to believe that he or she would allow himself or herself to be in an abusive relationship—in a controlling relationship, maybe, but not an abusive one. For many victims, being abused and controlled is what they know and what they often believe they deserve. However, just because the behavior is normal for them in a relationship does not mean it's healthy. It is important to realize that even without physical violence, a relationship may still be considered abusive. Emotional and mental abuse are still abuse, especially when they are used in a pattern of behavior to control, manipulate, or coerce the other partner.

Victims are not weak, nor are perpetrators strong. We live in a victim-blaming and victim-shaming culture, but truly many of those judged to be victims are really survivors. Getting up every day and functioning in life with hurt, pain, and often fear takes a great deal of strength and courage. People who are victimized over a long period of time are often traumatized, depressed, anxious, and perhaps even struggling with addiction. Imagine knowing that the person you love and trusted most in world were violating you and making you feel worthless, helpless, and afraid. Imagine being more afraid to leave than to stay—and with good reason. Research shows that 70 percent of victims get killed when they're leaving the relationship (Lawson 2003). How then would staying be the victim's fault? Victims don't choose abusive relationships; they pick romantic partners who sweep them off their feet, only to see those partners apparently change once they're hooked. Then the abuse begins. As their worlds get turned upside down and backward, the prince becomes a frog.

Abusive partners are bullies who control their partners with fear, hurtful comments, and isolation from support systems and other resources. They always need to be right and to win. Healthy relationships are partnerships. You can't have a partnership when one person has all the power, and the other has or believes she or he has none. That is a relational dictatorship, not a partnership.

Please note that all scenarios and characters in this book are fictional composites of real stories. They are written for illustrative purposes only.

PRETEST: MYTHS AND TRUTHS QUIZ

Before you begin reading, take this quiz and see how much you know about domestic violence. Answers are in the back of the book (chapter 12), but don't peek. Read the book, and then take this quiz again before you check the answers. Good luck!

Directions

Circle *myth* or *truth* next to each sentence.

1. Myth or truth: The victim always does something to provoke the abusive partner's violence.
2. Myth or truth: Children who are not primary victims of domestic violence are not really affected by domestic violence.
3. Myth or truth: Most batterers simply lose control during violent incidents and do not know what they're doing.
4. Myth or truth: When a couple is having a domestic violence problem, this just means the couple has a bad relationship. Often it's poor communication that is the problem.
5. Myth or truth: Domestic violence is often triggered by stress, such as the loss of a job or some financial or marital problem.

6. Myth or truth: Most real domestic violence only occurs in poor, minority, and/or trailer park communities.
7. Myth or truth: The use of intoxicating substances, such as drugs and/or alcohol, causes domestic violence.
8. Myth or truth: Just because violence occurs once in an intimate partner relationship does not mean it will happen again.
9. Myth or truth: Victims of domestic violence must like and/or provoke the abuse. If not, they would refuse to take it and just leave.
10. Myth or truth: Men are victims of domestic violence as often as women, even if they don't report it.
11. Myth or truth: Domestic violence is a less serious problem—less lethal—than "real" violence, such as street crimes.
12. Myth or truth: Where there is domestic violence, both parties are participants and are therefore responsible for the violence. For this reason, both parties are also responsible for stopping the violence.

When you retake this quiz after reading the first ten chapters of this book, see how many, if any, of your answers change. Then read chapter 12, "No More Myths: Truths Revealed," to check your answers.

What Is Domestic Violence?

Just because you can't get arrested for it does not mean it's not domestic violence—or that it does not count!

Domestic violence isn't always fully understood, and its definitions and perceptions vary. Many believe that such relationships must include physical violence, involvement of law enforcement, and/or an arrest. This is not true. Although some do, many do not. Understanding the true dynamics of domestic violence incudes understanding both the clinical and legal definitions. Legal definitions of domestic violence vary by state. In the state of Florida, where I live, domestic violence is legally defined as "any assault, aggravated assault, battery, aggravated battery, sexual assault, sexual battery, stalking, aggravated stalking, kidnapping, false imprisonment, or any criminal offense resulting in physical injury or the death of one family or household member by another family or household member" [Section 741.28(2), Florida Statutes (2017)]. Just because some types of abuse are legal doesn't mean they are ethical or healthy. Nor does it mean these behaviors don't count as domestic violence.

It's also important to remember that even when people are arrested for domestic violence, they are not always convicted. That doesn't mean that the violence didn't happen or doesn't matter or

1

didn't count. Sometimes there just isn't enough evidence to prove it happened. And sometimes the victim refuses to press charges out fear, love, or self-blame. Sadly, the legal system isn't always the *justice* system. Also, victims are often afraid to testify against their partners and don't show up in court. The legal mantra here is "no face, no case." When that happens, there is no legal action or consequences, but the event still counts as domestic violence.

Dominic and Violet
Dominic controlled everything Violet did. He controlled where she went, what she wore, whom she spoke to—he even controlled what she ate. After all, she had gained eight pounds since they had met, and he was not going to have a fat wife.   When they met, Dominic had been so charming. He was handsome and said all the right things. He would say, "You're so smart and so beautiful; I can't believe you're mine." At first Violet loved to hear these words, and she believed them.   Two weeks after they met, Dominic and Violet were saying, "I love you." Three months later, they were living together. Violet thought that Dominic's words were so wonderful and loving; they were music to her ears! As time went on, Dominic continued to refer to Violet as "his," as though she were a possession that belonged to him, but he no longer called her beautiful or smart. On the contrary, he frequently told her that she was "fat and stupid" and that if she ever left him, no one would ever want her. Violet began to feel as if Dominic was doing her a favor by staying with her, because he made her believe she was undesirable and worthless. In addition, she began to feel more like a possession than a partner.

When they met, Violet had had so many friends. Girls' night out had been her only relief from a grueling week. She was a nurse in an understaffed hospital and frequently picked up the slack whenever anyone called in. By the time Friday night rolled around, she couldn't wait to go out with the girls to socialize and let off some steam. As soon as she and Dominic moved in together, all that stopped. Dominic told her, "No girlfriend of mine is gonna go whoring around town with a bunch of drunk women." Violet would try to explain that that was not how it was, but Dominic refused to listen. He would always say, "I know you'd rather be home with your man," kiss her on the cheek, and then walk away.

The National Coalition Against Domestic Violence defines domestic violence as "willful intimidation, physical assault, battery, sexual assault, and/or other abusive behavior as part of a systematic pattern of power and control perpetrated by one intimate partner against another. It includes physical violence, sexual violence, psychological violence, and emotional abuse" (National Coalition Against Domestic Violence, 2017).

Domestic violence does not have to be physical to be abuse; nor does it have to be physical to hurt. Physical violence bruises the body; emotional/psychological violence bruises the soul and/or the spirit. Just because the perpetrator cannot legally be arrested or held accountable for emotional or psychological abuse doesn't mean that it didn't happen or doesn't count. An abusive relationship is one in which one partner doesn't feel she or he has a voice, or a choice, in the relationship or in decisions relating to his or her life (or sometimes both).

Abuse is a pattern of behavior. It is not an isolated incident or event. It does not have to be physical. A violent partner is just that: violent. An abusive partner is one who engages in a pattern of controlling, coercive, purposeful, isolating, and manipulative behaviors in order to attain or maintain control over the other partner.

Clint and Clara
Everyone was always telling Clara that Clint was such a great guy and that she was such a lucky woman. Clint was a successful businessman. He was handsome and always treated everyone with kindness and respect—at least in public. At home Clint was different. He was always putting Clara down. Clint would threaten, "You are my wife, and if I can't have you, nobody will. I'll make sure of that!" Whenever Clara disagreed with him, Clint told Clara she was "crazy" and that she didn't know what she was talking about. He knew she feared abandonment above all else, so he would often threaten to file for divorce, hire the "best, most expensive attorney," and get custody of the kids. He would tell her, "It will be easy, because you're crazy, and no judge in their right mind would let you have custody of my kids!" She was petrified of him and feared that no one would ever believe her if she shared what he was really like and what was going on behind closed doors. Clara cried every day, feeling stuck, isolated, and afraid.

Substance Abuse and Domestic Violence

Although there is a high correlation between alcohol, or other substance abuse, and battering, it is not a causal relationship. Batterers use drinking as one of many excuses for their violence and as a way to place the responsibility for their violence elsewhere.

Many people drink and/or take drugs but do not batter their partners. Just because a person batters while drunk or high does not necessarily mean that the person's relationship is abusive. It means they only batter *while*—not *because*—they are drunk or high. The drug (or alcohol) removes the filter.

Frequently, partners who are emotionally and mentally abusive while sober become physically abusive when drunk or high. If drugs and alcohol caused abusive battering behavior, then everyone who drank or used drugs would abuse his or her partner, and that is just not the case. Alcohol and drugs often escalate the lethality of the violence, but they do not *cause* the battering.

Often people who have no control over their drug and/or alcohol use try to control their partners instead. Substance abuse and domestic violence are both important clinical issues and must be addressed in treatment, but they must also be addressed as separate co-occurrent issues.

It is important to note that there are exceptions regarding alcohol and/or substance use/abuse and domestic violence. For example, some people are allergic or have violent chemical reactions to alcohol or to certain drugs, especially when alcohol and is being taken in conjunction with prescription and/or non-prescription medications.

Samantha and Sam

Samantha was pleading with the police officer, "He only hit me because he was drunk; he really didn't mean it. He just had a little too much to drink. He needs to get help for his drinking. He is a really good guy when he's sober. The alcohol turns him into someone else. It's not his fault." She forgot that when Sam is sober, he may not hit her, but he is abusive. He puts her down, calls her names, doesn't listen to or consider her opinions, and always needs to win and be right. He tells her everything is her fault. Sam takes no responsibility for himself or his actions, Sam blames Samantha, and Samantha blames the booze—and the cycle goes around and around.

Mental Health and Domestic Violence

Like substance abuse, a mental health diagnosis does not *cause* domestic violence. There are millions of people worldwide with a variety of mental health diagnoses who don't try to control, batter, or abuse their partners. Domestic violence is a learned behavior. When children grow up in a controlling and abusive environment, they learn that control, fear, and intimidation are the ways to have power and get your needs met and that "might is right." Normal isn't healthy, and healthy isn't normal.

Abusive and controlling partners are not crazy and are seldom psychotic. Most are fully aware of what they are doing. They use purposefully manipulative and coercive behavior that is designed to get what they want. If the abusive behavior were caused by a mental illness, then everyone with a mental illness would try to control or batter his or her partner, and that simply does not happen. In addition, victims commonly report that when their abusive partners are out in public, "It's like she [or he] is another person." Often victims of domestic violence describe their partners as a "Dr. Jekyll and Mr./Ms. Hyde." If mental illness were causing the abusive and controlling behaviors, the batterer would not be able to control it in front of other people.

Victims, on the other hand, often hear from their abusive partners that they are crazy, loco, or whacked in the head—so much so that they begin to believe it. Generally, it is the situation and the relationship that are so-called crazy, not the victim. Depression, anxiety, and post-traumatic stress disorder are common among victims of domestic violence (self-medicating addictive behaviors are also common). More often than not, these mental health issues are not because victims are crazy but are instead a result of having been victimized and often traumatized by abusers whom they loved and trusted. In addition, having been isolated and disempowered, they often lack healthy boundaries, tools, coping mechanisms, and support systems—a lack that causes them to feel helpless, hopeless, stuck, and afraid. If this sounds like you or someone you know or care about, I would ask that you (or your friend/loved one) get professional help from a licensed clinical professional who understands the dynamics and impact of domestic violence and its related trauma. If finances are an issue, many domestic violence centers and shelters offer individual outpatient counseling at no or minimal charge. Check your state's resources online, or visit the website for the National Coalition against Domestic Violence for more information. Counseling is often helpful for men and women who have been victims of domestic violence because it helps empower them, support them, educate them, and heal the pain and trauma of living and loving (or having lived and loved) in an abusive relationship.

Menna and Heath
Heath is always telling Menna that she a "crazy, fat ass, psycho bitch." He is so mentally and emotionally abusive that she would tell her doctor, "I know that there is something wrong with me. I cry all the time, I can't sleep, and I'm losing my mind, but I don't want to take any medication because Heath will use it against me in court and take my kids away from me. He already told me that if I try to leave him, he's gonna hire the best, most expensive lawyers and tell them how crazy I am and then take my kids away from me." Menna feels afraid (even though she doubts Health would ever physically hurt her), hopeless, and trapped. She is not mentally ill. She has been traumatized. She is struggling with depression and/or anxiety related to her victimization, but she is not crazy.

Bobby and Betty

Betty couldn't take it anymore. She told Bobby that she was "done" and wanted a divorce. They continued to argue, and then, uncharacteristically, Bobby walked away and into another room. Bobby called 911 and told the operator that he'd told Betty he wanted a divorce and that she'd gone went "crazy" and threatened to kill herself. He told them she had a prescription for Xanax and had threated to take the whole bottle. He told the operator that she had a history of depression and anxiety and that he feared for her safety. When the emergency personnel arrived, Betty denied the allegations about her wanting to harm herself, but Bobby was very convincing and she was extremely emotional. Not knowing what the truth was, and knowing she was on medication for depression and anxiety, the law enforcement officer said, "Better safe than sorry." Betty was "Baker Acted," meaning she underwent an emergency involuntary commitment to a residential facility. She was then transferred to an inpatient psychiatric facility as a result. Was this mental illness or manipulation?

Debbie and Damien

Debbie was tired of all the abuse and of being told that she was "a stupid, no good, fat, and lazy loser." She was told this first by her mother and now by her husband. He controlled everything she did, where she went, who she was, what she wore—*everything*! She struggled with depression and anxiety, and her therapist had recently discussed her having symptoms of post-traumatic stress disorder (PTSD). Debbie took a bottle of pills. Her husband tried to call all morning, but she didn't pick up the phone. He was sure she was having an affair. He left work and angrily drove home. Debbie was dead. Next to her was a note: "Damien, you have had control over my whole life, but you will *not* have control over my death. Goodbye!"

What Domestic Violence Is Not

False Allegations

Now that we've defined what an abusive relationship is, let's look at what it is not. An abusive relationship is not and should not be a way for non-victims to make false domestic violence allegations against their current or former partners, spouses, or co-parents in order to get a leg up in the legal and court systems. People who claim to be victims of domestic violence to get an injunction for protection (IFP), also known as a restraining order, in order to get primary custody of the children or the house, are controlling, manipulative, and coercive. They are the abusers!

Lucy and Larry

Larry and Lucy were married for twelve years. For most of their marriage, Lucy thought Larry was a great guy. Two months after their twelfth anniversary, Lucy began to tell her friends that she "just wasn't feeling it anymore." She cheated on Larry with Leon, a man she worked out with at the gym. When Larry found out that Lucy was having an affair, he got angry, called Lucy names, and threw a sandwich against the wall. Lucy went to the courthouse and reported that she was in an abusive relationship and in fear for her safety, and she filed for a divorce and a restraining order. When filling out the paperwork, she reported that her marriage to Larry was "violent and abusive" and that she was in fear for her safety.

Assholes and Bitches

Just because an intimate partner is an asshole or a bitch does not mean that he or she is an abuser. Likewise, a person who occasionally says mean or thoughtless things to or about his or her partner is not necessarily an abuser. By definition, abusive relationships include a pattern of manipulative and coercive behaviors. Isolated inappropriate behaviors and the people who exhibit them are inappropriate, but that does not does always mean that the person who exhibits these behaviors is an abuser.

Ashton and Bianca
Bianca and Ashton have been having trouble in their marriage for the past year. Ashton likes to go out with the boys, have a few drinks, and flirt with the bartenders and waitresses. Although Bianca says that Ashton has plenty of energy when he is out at the clubs, at home he seldom gets off the sofa. She is turned off by what she calls his "lazy-ass attitude" and behavior. Ashton got laid off a year and a half ago, and he refuses to look for work or help around the house. Bianca works more than forty hours a week and takes care of the kids and the house. Ashton only wants to spend time with her when he wants to have sex. Bianca is too tired to be interested in sex— especially with a man who "flirts with anything in a skirt!" She tells him that he is "an abusive player who treats her like a slave" and that one day she is going to leave him; when she does, it'll be his "own damn fault."

Also, just because a good relationship or marriage is over and the separation or divorce is ugly does not mean that the whole relationship was abusive. Many times, good relationships run their course, and in the midst of a breakup or divorce, they get ugly (especially if the breakup was a result of infidelity). Ugly divorces are usually different from abusive relationships; they can be toxic and unhealthy without being abusive. That being said, abusive marriages that end often end in abusive and sometimes dangerous divorces.

Communication versus Control

Vanessa and Victor
Vanessa complained to her therapist, "We're always fighting. He says all I do is push his buttons every time we try to talk. I always make him so mad. We obviously have a communication problem." Victor understands what Vanessa is telling him; he just refuses to acknowledge or validate it. Victor believes that if Vanessa's thoughts or ideas do not match his, they are not worth responding to or validating. In fact, Victor "punishes" Vanessa with silence because she has the nerve to have her own opinion. Victor believes the only ideas or opinions that matter are his. Vanessa doesn't realize that this is not just "a problem with communication"; it is a problem with control. It's not that the communication isn't clear. It's just one-sided. Victor's behavior has fallen into a pattern of abuse.

All couples experience conflicts. Conflict is a normal and healthy part of relationships. It becomes abusive when one partner must always win and be right, and as a result, the conflict often escalates into verbal or physical violence. In an abusive relationship, even if a victim speaks, he or she seldom feels as though his or her thoughts and feelings are heard, respected, or validated. As a result, victims often stop talking and sharing, hoping that will make the fighting stop. In a healthy relationship, couples can have conflict without violence, and when there is a conflict, they work to solve to solve the problem—not to win an argument.

Angel and Annie

Angel just threw Annie up against the wall and tried to choke her. He knew just where to put his hands so that he wouldn't leave a mark. The neighbors heard her screaming and called law enforcement. Annie was scared that if she told the whole truth about what was really going on, Angel would be even angrier and she would "get in trouble." She did not understand that it was his behavior that got him in trouble, not her. When the police came, she told them, "He didn't mean it. He has a problem with his anger. He doesn't need to be arrested; he needs anger management." It is interesting that when Angel is at work he doesn't have any problem with his anger. He is great with customers, coworkers, and bosses. They all love him. Annie writes in her journal that he is like Dr. Jekyll and Mr. Hyde, but she is afraid to say it to anyone out loud. She is afraid of making him mad and of getting punished.

Codependency versus Control

Unlike partners in an abusive relationship, enablers and codependents share control. *Codependency* is a term that is often used to describe relationships in which one person struggles with some type of addiction or addictive behavior and his or her partner enables that behavior by continuing to rescue him or her. As a result, the addicted partner never experiences the consequences of his or her actions.

Although the enabler might appear to be controlling or even the victim of an abusive relationship, the enabler's behavior is based on an unhealthy love or attachment—not fear or powerlessness. On the contrary, the enabler feels empowered because he or she feels needed and believes, "As long as you need me, you'll never leave me." A victim of domestic violence is not codependent; she or he is fully dependent on her or his partner. The abusive partner has all the power in the relationship and the victim has none—or very little. The prefix *co* means two, meaning that both partners are dependent on each other. Often codependent partners refer to each other as "my other" or "my better half." This is symbolic because codependent partners feel incomplete without the other partner. Each partner needs her or his other half to feel whole. (Please note: I said *feel* whole—not *be* whole.)

It is important to understand that just because a person is in a relationship with an addicted partner doesn't necessarily make the person an enabler. The person might be a victim.

Cody and Connie

Cody and Connie have been married for twenty-five years. Connie is an alcoholic and has been drinking since she was thirteen years old. Cody often makes excuses for her, cares for her, and says that he puts up with her inappropriate behaviors because "I love her" and "she needs me." Cody is a caretaker and needs to feel needed. Their relationship works because Connie under functions, and Cody over functions. Each partner brings an unhealthy balance to the other. One is needy, and the other needs to feel needed. Each partner has a role. Each person has half the power (even though sometimes it doesn't appear or feel that way to either of them), and together the two halves make a whole. This is why they each refer to the other partner as "my other half"; without the other partner, each only feels like half a person. When they are not together, it leaves a hole.

Anger versus Control

A person's inability to control his or her anger is not the same as using aggressive outbursts as an excuse to control his or her

13

partner. Anger and so-called "problems with anger management" are not exclusively the causes of domestic violence. Many (too many) batterers and victims blame domestic violence (physical battering) on problems with "anger management." If a person can control his or her anger at work or with friends at restaurants but can't do the same at home, then he or she does not have a problem with "anger management"—he or she has a problem with control.

Violence and anger are related only in that when a person feels he or she is losing control of the other partner, he or she gets angry and often violent. A person struggling with with anger management would not be able to control who the recipient of his or her unleashed anger was; nor would he or she be able to make sure that the bruises always ended up in places where no one could see them. That being said, there are people who have a problem managing both their anger and their desire to control their partners.

Mental illness is seldom the cause of domestic violence, but it often triggers or exacerbates mental health problems, such as depression, anxiety, and PTSD, for its victims.

Domestic violence is a learned behavior in which one person controls, coerces, and manipulates the other. It is not *caused* by alcohol or substance abuse or mental illness. (There are a few exceptions, such as drug reactions or interactions with other drugs or alcohol, allergies, and violent psychotic episodes.) Although it's often easier to blame the drugs or alcohol, more often than not it's the person's need to control his or her partner that causes the aggressive behavior. Generally, it's not that the aggressor can't control his or her behavior; the truth is more likely that the aggressor chooses not to.

Again, please remember that just because a person is violent when drunk or high *does not mean* that she or he is controlling or abusive *because* she or he is drunk or high. The same goes for mental illnesses: just because someone is struggling with a mental illness and may be violently and aggressively acting out does not necessarily mean she or he is attempting to control her or his partner. The dynamic of the partner who is violent because of mental illness and active psychosis is very different from the one described within these chapters—unless, of course, the violent partner is both mentally ill and controlling and abusive. In that case, it is the need to control and abuse that are co-occurrent. The mental illness is *not* causing the controlling abusive behavior.

 ## Types of Abuse in an Intimate Partner Relationship

The National Coalition of Domestic Violence defines domestic violence as the "willful intimidation, physical assault, battery, sexual assault, and/or other abusive behavior as part of a systematic pattern of power and control perpetrated by one intimate partner against another. It includes physical violence, sexual violence, psychological violence, and emotional abuse" (NCADV, 2017).

Caitlyn and Caleb
Caitlyn's husband, Caleb, had just been arrested for domestic violence and was being transported to jail as she was being transported to the emergency room. When she arrived at the emergency room, she had a large gash on her cheek from being thrown into the wall and into a mirror. A domestic violence advocate was called in to meet with her. As the advocate was talking to her, she asked Caitlyn, "Was this the worst thing that he has ever done to you?" Her reply was no. The advocate then asked, "What was the worst thing he ever did to you?" She said, "He slept with a prostitute and told me that the sex with her was better than sex with me."

> For Caitlyn, the wound on her heart (and spirit) the day her husband said those emotionally battering words was more painful than having five stitches in her cheek. Regardless of what others may think about how crazy her reaction was, this was Caitlyn's perception of what Caleb had done to her. Isn't it ironic that he could be held legally accountable for the physical violence but not the emotional or psychological violence that she described as more painful?

Domestic violence is often thought of as physical violence in relationships. The term *verbal abuse* is common, and many people understand what that is, but in controlling, abusive relationships there are a number of ways that one partner controls the other. They include physical abuse, emotional abuse, mental or psychological abuse, sexual abuse, and destruction of property or pets. They each have an impact. In combination, they form toxic and effective ways for one partner to exert control over another. Not only do these forms of abuse keep control with the abuser, but they also ensure that the partner doesn't leave the relationship and take away the control that so often is confused with—or at some point seems to replace—love.

Physical Abuse

Physical abuse is any type of physical behavior used with the intention of controlling another person, such as pushing, slapping, shoving, stabbing, or pulling hair. Physical abuse is used by the abusive partner in order to control the other. A victim of abuse will tell you that physical abuse is no better or worse than other types of abuse. When it happens, victims of physical abuse generally know that it is abuse and that it is against the law. Legal consequences, although often minimal, can follow this type of abuse. This is not always the case with more manipulative, coercive, and insidious types of abuse.

Victims who have been physically abused often say that their partners have anger issues, but a person who can control her or his anger around everyone other than her or his partner does not have anger issues; she or he has control issues.

As mentioned earlier, but can't be reinforced enough, domestic violence is more about the desire to control one's partner than the inability to manage or control one's anger. People who have a true inability to control their anger generally have a significant medical issue that is usually neurological or psychiatric. As with diabetes or cancer, a person can't have a medical condition at home and not at work or out at social events. A person either has a medical or psychiatric issue, or he or she doesn't. The same is true for anger. If a person can control his or her anger at work, with friends, or in front of a therapist, then he or she can control his or her anger but chooses not to. Such a person wants to control his or her partner, not anger.

Also, a person who truly has a problem with anger and related behaviors is not going to be able to control where he or she leaves bruises. Yet often victims who have been physically abused have bruises where clothes will be able to cover them. If a person can control where the bruises end up, she or he can control whether or not to put them there. Batterers who leave bruises where others can see them are more lethal, not just because they can't control their anger but also because they are beyond caring who knows that they are battering their partners.

Philip and Phyllis

Phyllis walked into her counselor's office with bruises on her arm and on her face. She told the counselor that her boyfriend, Philip, "accidentally" hit her when he was angry. She did not say anything about the bruises on her arm (which were partially covered by a long-sleeve shirt) that she got when Phil grabbed her and threw her up against a wall.

She said that it was "an accident" and that "he said he was sorry and that it will never happen again." Then she added, "It was my fault. I made him mad. I know he doesn't like it when I go out with my friends after work. He was working late, so I didn't think it would matter that much, but boy was I wrong! I won't do that again!"

Before Philip, Phyllis's ex-boyfriend, Paul, was never physically abusive but was abusive to her in other ways (emotionally and mentally). When they broke up, he told her, "You were such a waste of my time. You're so lucky I never hit you" and then added "but maybe I should have."

Phyllis knew, because of the physical violence, that her relationship was abusive. She believed she had the power to change it, make it stop, or make it better, as long as she didn't "make him mad." Having been "beaten down" before in an emotionally and mentally abusive relationship prior to her relationship with Philip, she was use assuming blame and trying to change her behavior rather than have Philip change or be accountable for his.

Emotional Abuse

Emotional abuse is not an isolated behavior or event. It goes well beyond a mean or inappropriate comment. Ongoing abusive comments attack a person's self-esteem and emotions, such as when one partner repeatedly calls the other stupid, fat, ugly, lazy, worthless, etc. Unlike physical abuse, the bruises are on the inside and can't be seen. They are what one might call an inside ouch. That does not make them less real or less painful. Emotional abuse is not against the law, and to many victims, it is unrecognizable as abuse. Over a period of time, emotional abuse is a form of brainwashing. Unlike with the POWs, strangers do not do the brainwashing; a person the victim loves, trusts, and may even have a child or children with commits this emotional abuse. This, along with isolation and other types of coexisting abuse, makes the abuser's words that much more powerful and believable. Bruises from emotional abuse are not visible. They are on the victim's feelings, heart, spirit, and perceptions of self-worth.

Emmitt and Emma
Emma and Emmitt meet online shortly after Emma has separated from her first husband, who left her for a woman seventeen years younger than she is. Emma was a prima ballerina until she was twenty-one, when she chose marriage and motherhood over a career. Without a husband and two daughters, who are now grown, Emma feels lost and empty. In walks Emmitt. He tells her that he can't believe any man would choose someone younger over her. He tells her she is beautiful, intelligent, and loyal. He adds, "Oh well, his loss is my gain." They spend every day and every night together from the time they meet until two months later, when Emmitt invites Emma to move in. "After all, we spend all our time together anyway. Why pay for an expensive closet just to keep your clothes?" Emmitt explains that she will not need "all that extra stuff that just reminds you of him anyway" and suggests she sells it all. She agrees, sells most of her furniture and household items, and moves in with him. At first it is great. They spend all their time together. He doesn't want her to work because it would take away from their time together. More importantly, he says, she "deserves to be taken care of." He begins to isolate her from her family and friends, and a year into their living together, she realizes that she had only spoken to family and friends at Easter and Christmas. Emmitt begins telling Emma what to do instead of asking her. He begins to complain about how she dresses and wears her hair and makeup and often tells her to change her clothes, telling her that she "looks like a ho."

He has slowly shifted from telling her that she is beautiful to telling her that her breasts are too small and her belly too big. Emma's self-esteem and body image begin to fall. She begins to dress in baggier clothes so that she will not look like she is trying to attract other men, and she becomes more and more self-conscious about her body. She has gained four pounds in the past eight months and wonders if it is really that noticeable. She is getting older, she acknowledges, and is probably losing muscle tone. She will have to go back to the gym, she decides, and soon!

Unlike Phyllis in the previous example, Emma (because Emmitt never hit her) does not even realize that she is in a controlling and abusive relationship.

Mental or Psychological Abuse

Mental or psychological abuse is when a controlling partner uses manipulation and/or coercion to get what she or he wants. She or he often plays head games and tries to make her or his partner feel crazy. Fear and intimation are also very frequently used forms of mental or psychological abuse. This type of abuse is often magnified when physical violence has been part of the relationship history; even without a history of physical violence, it is often a very frightening and effective method of control. Without words, the victim fears another beating or other form of punishment should she or he not do what the abusive partner says or wants. Like emotional abuse, psychological abuse is generally not against the law. It is often also very difficult to prove, as it comes down to "he said, she said." The abusive partner speaks and acts very differently in front of others and says that the victim is crazy when abuse is disclosed. While emotional abuse directly affects the heart (feelings, emotions, and self-esteem), mental abuse targets the mind (head games). The two are similar, and there are crossover phrases and behaviors, but they are not the same.

Miguel and Marcey

When Marcey met Miguel, she told all her friends that she had hit the jackpot. She had met her soul mate! He was everything she had prayed for. He was handsome, he was loving, he was kind, he was attentive, and he told her that he thought she was beautiful! From the time they met, they both knew that this was it! Six weeks into the relationship, Miguel asked Marcey to move in. He told her that he loved her and wanted to take care of her. Why should she pay "all that money" for an apartment when they were spending most of their nights together anyway? Marcey was not sure she was ready, but her lease was ending soon, so she agreed. As soon as she moved in, she noticed that things with Miguel began to change. He spoke differently to her, got angry more often, and didn't want her to spend time with any of her friends or family—especially her twin sister Marta, and they had been inseparable since birth! When Marcey and Miguel were in the car, he would often drive too fast to frighten or intimidate her. She would ask him to stop, but the more afraid she became, the faster he would drive. She would get so scared she would scream, "Stop the car! I wanna get out! *Please, please, let me out!*" Fearing she would leave him, he would say, "You are my girl, and if I can't have you, nobody will." He knew she had a fear of drowning, so Miguel told her if she ever tried to break up with him or leave the relationship, he would drive "right off the bridge and into the canal." Sometimes he would just add, "Nah, I wouldn't want to ruin my car because of you. I'll just throw you over the bridge and tell everyone you jumped." Although he would never have done it, she believed him.

Marcey was afraid to stay but more afraid to leave, even though he had never hit her. Miguel was manipulative and played "head games" with her. Miguel never hit Marcey, but he isolated her from her family and friends and told her she was a "stupid, fat ho" and that it was a good thing for her that he stayed with her, because "nobody else would want your sorry ass!" Miguel was able to control Marcey without physical violence. Marcey thought that people in abusive relationships got hit or punched by their partners Miguel had a very high degree of control over Marcey, but he never was physically abusive to her. As a result, she had no idea that she was in an emotionally and mentally abusive relationship.

For those who are into fitness or have fitness-minded partners, it is important to remember that eye rolling is not exercise. When it's a pattern of behavior in a relationship, it's a non-verbal way for one partner to communicate disgust and/or disregard for the other partner's words or actions.

Gaslighting

Gaslighting is a form of mental or psychological abuse. It's the technical term for what is more often referred to as crazy-making behavior. It's a psychological technique whereby one partner tries to manipulate or trick the other into questioning his or her sanity. In other words, it's a form of brainwashing. It happens over time. It does not make a person crazy, but it certainly can make him or her feel that way. Gaslighting gives more power to the abusive partner, over time making the victim feel crazy, unstable, and extremely vulnerable.

Gary and Gilda
Gary was always calling Gilda a "psycho crazy ass bitch." He was always hiding her things, especially her keys. After she looked for them for hours, he would put them on the kitchen table and tell her that they were there all along. Gilda would say, "I could swear they weren't there a few minutes ago!" Gary would laugh and say, "Yeah, that's it! They just appeared from out of nowhere and just jumped up onto the table!" In the morning he would frequently move her coffee from the kitchen table to the bathroom, telling her that she brought it with her when she was going in to take a shower. She would tell him she left it on the table in the kitchen, and he would respond, "Then how did it get in there you stupid bitch? You're losing your mind—if you even have one left to lose!" As Gary continued to gaslight Gilda, she began to question her own sanity, not his actions.

Destruction of Property or Hurting Pets

Destruction of property or pets is a form of mental or psychological abuse but is often given its own category of abuse. Often, abusive and controlling partners will not hit their partners; rather, they will hit the wall or the dog instead, the underlying message being, "This time it's the dog, but the next time, it's gonna be you!" or "You'd better behave, or the dog will get hurt—and it will be all your fault!" After enduring years of abuse (or sometimes even at the start of the abuse), victims often care more about protecting their animals from physical harm than they do themselves.

Doug and Donna
Donna and Doug have been living together for seven years. Donna says she loves Doug, but she is very concerned about his so-called anger problem. Every time he gets angry with her, he shoves or kicks her dog. The interesting thing is that they both have a dog, but every time Doug gets angry, the only dog he kicks or hurts is hers, even if his is in the room with them and he has to go into another room to find her dog. Donna wonders if Doug can't control his anger, why is it only her dog he that kicks and hurts? This type of violence isn't just about anger; it's about control. Once Doug picked up the dog and threw her across the room. He was not only physically abusing the dog but psychologically abusing Donna as well.

Sexual Abuse or Coercion in a Relationship

Whether a couple is married, living together, or just dating, any type of sexual activity that is forced or not consensual (such as forcing a partner to dress sexier than he or she is comfortable with, forcing or tricking a partner into pregnancy, withholding sex as a means of punishing a partner, or exerting control) is a form of sexual abuse in a relationship.

Sid and Sophie
Sophie and Sid had been married for three years. During the first six months of their marriage, he began treating her differently, as if she belonged to him. He would say things like, "These are my golf clubs, my car, and my wife." Sophie felt more like a possession than a partner. When Sid would go out with the boys, Sophie was seldom invited, and when she asked to go, Sid always told her no. When he got home, he not only wanted to have sex, but he wanted oral sex.

Sophie had been sexually abused by a so-called family friend from the time she was seven until she was twelve. During that time, she had been forced to have oral sex that made her gag and then vomit after he ejaculated in her mouth. As a result of this childhood trauma, Sophie is unable to have oral sex without it triggering past trauma and related emotions. Even when Sid had not been drinking, he would tell Sophie that he really liked oral sex and would say, "If you won't do it, I'll find someone who will." Sophie feared losing Sid to another woman. She would do whatever it took to keep him. Every time she tried giving him oral sex, she choked, cried, and shut down. When Sophie was no longer willing to try, Sid began to force her to have oral sex by grabbing her hair and pushing and pulling her head down until he was ready to either stop and have intercourse or ejaculate. Thinking it would be easier, Sophie would try to cooperate with Sid's "requests" for oral sex. If she felt she had a choice she would have declined, but she was afraid of what Sid would do to her if she didn't cooperate. She prayed for it to be over and just got through it. Cooperation is not the same as free will consent. Sex without free will consent by a legal standard is sexual abuse or sexual assault.

Giving a partner a sexually transmitted disease (STD) is not always sexual abuse. It is only sexual abuse when the partner who has an STD doesn't tell his or her partner that he or she has been infected. Sexual partners have a right to informed consent. If a person knows she or he is infected with an STD and doesn't inform her or his partner, that's sexual abuse. Just because a person consents to sex doesn't mean the person is consenting to being exposed to an STD. This is especially important to remember for those partners who no longer need to worry about pregnancy and as a result don't use condoms.

Stan and Stacie

Stacie was fifty-nine years old and had only been with three men before meeting Stan: her college boyfriend, a post-college boyfriend, and a husband of nineteen years whom she'd divorced seven months prior. After months of dating, Stan told Stacie that he'd had a vasectomy twelve years so there was no longer a need to use condoms. Stacie asked that she and Stan get tested before having sex without a condom. His response was, "I'm sixty-two years old. I'm not some young stud. What type of guy do you think I am anyway?" So she ignored her gut instinct and had unprotected sex with him. Stacie got herpes. Stan had known that he had herpes. He purposely gave it Stacie, hoping that she would be too embarrassed or ashamed to have sex with anyone else or to leave him. Stacie cried and cried when she found out. Just as Stan had hoped, she felt stuck and that nobody would ever want her again. After all, she was so called damaged goods. Even if the sex appears to be consensual, knowingly giving someone an STD is sexual abuse.

When sex is used as a form of manipulation in a relationship, that too is sexual abuse. Lying about use of birth control, saying that he will pull out and then doesn't (not a reliable form of birth control in the first place), or refusing to use birth control and forcing sex anyway are all forms of sexual abuse in a relationship.

Manuel and Mandy

Mandy and Manuel have been together four years. Mandy wanted to get married and have a baby, but for Manuel marriage was not an option. Manuel's mother had been married and divorced five times before Manuel's eighteenth birthday.

He told Mandy that he loved her, but he did not believe in marriage and would never marry her. They have been struggling with their relationship for about a year and half. Mandy is afraid of losing Manuel and, as a result, has become very controlling. She believes that if they were to have a baby and become a family rather than just a couple, then he would have to stay. In spite of the fact that they talked about waiting until he gets out of graduate school to get pregnant, Mandy stops taking her birth control pills with the intention of getting pregnant and trapping Manuel into staying with her. She is using sex in a coercive and manipulative manner to control Manuel and the situation. Even though the sex is consensual, the coercion and manipulation related to it are not. This is a form of sexual abuse in a relationship.

Environmental Abuse

Environmental abuse in a relationship is when the abusive partner uses or controls the other partner's environment and support system to be better able to control him or her (such as using isolation, sabotaging the victim's support system, or not allowing or sabotaging partner's employment). This type of abuse is usually fueled by being jealous (frequently accusing the victim of having or wanting to have sex with someone else), not wanting one's partner to have a support system other than the abusive partner, and fearing that if one doesn't keep his or her partner on a (metaphoric) leash, the partner will run away or leave.

Evan and Ethan
Evan and Ethan met through a gay online dating service, and Evan got Ethan to agree to move in with him just six weeks

after they met. Evan gushed, "I am so in love with you that I just want to spend every waking minute I can with you!" Ethan gave up his apartment and moved in with Evan.

Ethan's parents had no trouble with their son being gay, but they were very leery and disapproving of Ethan's quickly moving relationship with Evan and told him so. Three months after they began living together, Evan moved Ethan from Boston to Baltimore. The quickly moving relationship soon included moving away. It was after they got to Baltimore that Ethan began to notice that Evan was very jealous. He would get upset when Ethan talked with his old friends and roommates or other guys he worked with at the restaurant. Evan would say, "I love you so much. I just want you all to myself." Ethan had never felt so loved and cared about. As time went on, Evan became more and more controlling. He would call Ethan at work, and if he didn't answer within three rings, Evan would show up to see whom Ethan was talking to and what he was doing. He would always start an argument before Ethan went to work, causing him to be late and ultimately causing him to get fired. Ethan became financially dependent on Evan. Ethan's parents were still in Boston, and the longer he was with Evan, the less he saw and even had contact with them. Every time he would bring up wanting to call his parents, Evan would tell him, "Don't bother with that now; call them later. Come here and talk to me. I'm your family now, and you're mine." Ethan didn't want to hear his parents say, "I told you so," so he decided that he would call them when things got better. He had no idea they would only get worse—much worse. Environmental abuse, although not illegal, is unhealthy and unethical, and it often sets the stage for the victim to feel trapped, unsupported, and alone.

Regardless of the abusive partner's type of abuse, his or her catalyst is to gain or maintain control over his or her partner, the victim.

3   Dynamics of Domestic Violence

Part 1: Power and Control in Intimate Partner Relationships

D omestic violence, especially as it relates to manipulation, coercion, and control, takes many different forms, which can make it difficult to determine when it is occurring. There are three main components to the dynamics of domestic violence: power and control, types of abuse, and the cycle of violence.

Cole and Ling
Ling and Cole have been married for twenty-five years. Ling has a bachelor of science in nursing. She met Cole a month before graduation and married him six months later. She has never worked outside the home. Cole is the so-called man of the house. He makes the rules, and she is expected to follow them "or else."

Ling had been looking forward to finally getting a job and going to work once all three children were in school, but Cole refuses to let her work even after their youngest has graduated high school. He also refuses to let her spend time out with her friends. Cole is the breadwinner and has the only income.

He pays all the bills. When Ling goes shopping, she has to ask him for the money, buy only what is on a list approved by him, and give him the change and the receipts. Cole has all the power in the relationship, and Ling has none. There is no balance—only control.

Power and Control Wheel

The Duluth Model Power and Control Wheel, created by Domestic Abuse Intervention Project in Duluth, Minnesota, is a helpful tool for understanding the overall pattern of abusive and violent behaviors in relationships (Domestic Abuse Intervention Project, 2017). Often one or more violent incidents will be accompanied by an array of these and often other types of abuse. They are less easily identified yet firmly establish a pattern of intimidation and control in the relationship.

In 1984, staff at the Domestic Abuse Intervention Project, began developing curricula for working with groups of men who batter and victims of domestic violence. They needed a way to create descriptions of batterers and of victims for practitioners in the criminal justice field. In order to understand the dynamics of domestic violence, they formed focus groups of women who had been battered to share their stories and help create the data. The project then documented the most common abusive behaviors or tactics that were reported in the men's focus groups. The tactics the staff chose for the wheel were those that were most universally experienced by victims of domestic violence, who at the time were referred to as "battered women."

DOMESTIC ABUSE INTERVENTION PROGRAMS
202 East Superior Street
Duluth, Minnesota 55802
218-722-2781
www.theduluthmodel.org

Part 2: Types of Abuse in an Intimate Partner Relationship

Using Intimidation

Intimidation in a relationship is when one partner tries to control the other through fear—such as directing intimidating looks, actions, or gestures toward the other partner; smashing things; destroying the partner's property; abusing pets; and/or displaying weapons.

Tim and Ingrid

Every time Ingrid questioned something Tim said, he would get angry. If she asked to go out with her friends or threatened to leave him, he would smash his fist into the wall. If they were in the car, he would drive really fast to frighten and intimidate her. Ingrid would tell Tim she was scared, but he wouldn't stop until she said he was right or that she was sorry or that she would never say she was thinking about leaving him again. He would add, "If I can't have you, *nobody* will," and Ingrid just knew that he meant it.

Using Emotional Abuse

Emotional abuse in a relationship is when one partner puts the other partner down, making him or her feel bad about himself or herself. Emotional abuse leaves bruises on the inside, bruises on a person's feelings and sense of self-worth.

Emeril and Emily

Emeril was always telling Emily that she was a fat, ugly, and useless piece of shit and that it was a good thing he stayed with her, because no one else would want or tolerate her sorry ass. Even though she was a former beauty pageant winner and high school teacher, she believed him.

Using Isolation

Isolation in a relationship is when one partner controls whom the other partner sees and talks to, what the other person reads, where the other person goes, and his or her outside involvement, as well as when one partner uses jealousy to justify these actions.

This not only removes the victim from his or her support system, but it also removes the victim's ability to gain the perspective of a reality check regarding the control and manipulation going on in the relationship.

Ishmael and Isabel (Izzy)
Ishmael and Isabel got pregnant on their honeymoon. Ishmael told Izzy to quit her job and take it easy while she was pregnant. At the time she saw this as a gesture of love and support. After the baby was born, Ishmael suggested Izzy just stay home and take care of the baby; he would take care of everything else. The biggest thing that Ishmael took care of was removing Izzy's support system. He isolated her from her work peers and then from her friends and family. By the time the baby was six months old, Izzy's support system was gone, and she had no adult to hold onto—except Ishmael.

Minimizing, Denying, and Blaming

Minimizing, denying, and blaming happen in a relationship when one partner makes light of the abuse rather than taking the other partner's concerns about it seriously. Saying the abuse didn't happen, shifting responsibility for abusive behavior, or saying the partner caused it are all examples of this damaging behavior. Often the victim ends up taking responsibility for the abuse because the partner perpetrating it refuses to take responsibility and has told the victim over and over again that it is all his or her fault.

Minnie and Barney
After making a joke about her cooking, Barney would minimize Minnie's feelings by telling her to stop being so sensitive. When she would get more upset about his continued joking remarks, he would say that he didn't mean it *that* way, denying his hurtful and abusive intentions. Barney also had a habit of blaming her for his actions. Barney told Minnie that if she didn't make him so mad, he wouldn't have to scream and yell and sometimes push, shove, or hit her. He warned Minnie to stop pushing his buttons. It was that simple—or was it?

Using Children

Abusive partners often try to gain control by making their partners feel guilty about the children, using the children to relay messages, using visitation to harass their partners, and/or threatening to take the children away. The abusive partner often treats the children more like possessions than people.

Charlene and Charlie
Charlene had been struggling with depression and anxiety for years. Charlie was always telling Charlene that she was "a crazy, psycho bitch" and that if she tried to leave, he would make sure that the judge knew just how crazy she was so that he would get full custody. He would tell her the kids were his and that no one was going to take them from him. In addition, he would tell Charlie Jr. how much he loved Mommy and wanted to be with her but would also say that "Mommy is breaking up the family."

Using Male Privilege

Using male privilege in a relationship (when the victim is female) is when the abusive partner treats his victim like a servant, makes all the big decisions, acts like the master of the castle, and is the one to define men's and women's roles. This occurs most frequently with couples that are in what was once referred to as "traditional marriages," where the "I pay, I say" method is often the household way.

Malachai
Malachai personified male privilege. He believed that he was the man of the house and would proclaim loudly and proudly, "I am the man, the head of this household, and what I say goes".

Financial or Economic Abuse

Financial or economic abuse in a relationship is when one partner prevents the other from getting or keeping a job, makes the other ask for money, gives an allowance, takes the other's money, prevents the other from knowing about bank accounts and/or household bills or finances, and/or doesn't allow the other to have access to family income.

Finn and Edna
Edna was on Social Security disability due to an automobile accident followed by a number of unsuccessful back surgeries. Finn was a retired law enforcement officer. Edna's check went into a mutual bank account, but Finn held the checkbook and the password. After all, he believed he was better with money, and he paid all the bills. When Edna went shopping for food or household items or needed to put gas in her car,

Finn would give her money (or his credit card), but she needed to account for every cent she spent. He would count the change against the balance on the receipt, just to make sure she didn't "try to stash some money away for a rainy day." Even though Edna's name was on the account, she was not allowed access to it, the debit and credit card, or the checkbook, without Finn's knowledge or consent.

Coercion and Threats

Using coercion and threats in a relationship is when one partner makes and/or carries out threats to hurt the other partner, such as threatening to leave him or her, threatening to commit suicide, or threatening to report the victim to social services without cause. It is also when the abusive partner makes or forces the victim to drop charges against him or her, and/or forces the victim to use drugs or do illegal things.

Curt and Theresa

Curt told Theresa that he loved her and that she was his wife and belonged to him. No other man would ever have her. He "loved her to death." He would often tell her that if she left, he couldn't go on. He would tell her, "If you leave, I would kill myself, and then you would have to live with what _you_ did!" Sometimes he would add, "Or maybe I'll just take you and the kids with me. If we are not gonna live as a family, then we will die as a family."

Part 3: Cycle of Violence

The Three Stages of the Cycle of Violence

Abusive relationships often go around and around in what is referred to as the cycle of violence. The cycle, which was developed by Dr. Lenore Walker, has three stages: the tension building stage, the violent episode/incident or battering stage, and the honeymoon stage. This cycle is illustrated in the relationship of Veronica and Victor, which I will discuss in greater detail below.

Veronica and Victor
Veronica and Victor have been dating for three years. The first six months were magical. As time went on, the relationship got less magical and more controlling, but every so often the magic returned. Veronica noticed that the magical moments only seemed to appear after a fight, however.

The tension building stage. This is where the tension and stress build, and the emotional and/or mental (non-physical) violence occurs. During this stage, Veronica feels like she is "walking on egg shells," knowing something is going to happen but not knowing what or when. She describes it as "waiting for the other shoe to drop." She has a knot in her stomach when she waits for Victor to get home, knowing she will need to assess what type of mood he is in so she can know what type of night it's going to be and whether or not he may get angry again.

The violent episode (battering) stage. During this stage, the victim (and other members of the family) no longer need to wait for the other shoe to drop. This is when Victor is physically violent with

Veronica. Although he has slapped, pushed, choked, and shoved Veronica, he has never once left a bruise.

The honeymoon stage. The violent episode breaks the tension and then is generally followed by the honeymoon stage. The honeymoon stage is not about making up but sucking up. During this stage, the batterer knows that he or she has gone too far. The violent partner says and does whatever it takes to keep his or her partner from leaving, to get the partner to drop the charges if there are any, and to get the partner to return home if he or she has left. During this stage, Victor tells Veronica that he is sorry and promises, "It will never happen again. I just love you so much, and you make me so mad, but I forgive you. Let's go out for dinner and just have good time. I am so, so sorry. You know I would never hurt you on purpose. You just made me so mad." He offers to go to counseling and to take her out to a special dinner. Sometimes he brings her flowers (roses), gifts (jewelry), etc. Veronica wants to believe him and that this time it will be different, so she stays.

The honeymoon stage feeds into the fantasy and denial in the relationship, enabling the victim to thin, *This is the man (or woman) I fell in love with. He (or she) really does love me and is going to change. The relationship will go back to the way it was in the beginning, and we will be happy again.* The honeymoon stage lasts until the abusive partner knows that the victim has been sucked back into his or her manipulative web and is not going to leave the relationship or has returned home after leaving, or the time to testify in court against the perpetrator has past. Then the tension returns, and the cycle begins again. To return to Veronica and Victor, as soon as Veronica refers to him as "the old Victor, the one I feel in love with," the honeymoon is over, and they go back into the tension stage. The cycle begins again.

As time goes on, the tension and battering stages get longer and stronger, and the hopeful honeymoon stage gets shorter and weaker. In addition to the physical abuse, the victim also becomes badly beaten down. As time goes on, the batterer believes it is unlikely that the victim will leave because the victim fears no one will want her or him or that she or he will not be able to make it alone. The batterer no longer needs to manipulate and suck up to the victim. Eventually the battering incidents increase in frequency and lethality. If you recognize this pattern in your relationship, please seek out the help of a professional. Even if you are not ready to leave, you need information, support, and most importantly a safety plan. Even if you have never been hit or physically hurt in any way during the relationship, you still need a safety plan should you choose to leave later or need help understanding that you are not alone, crazy, or stuck.

Domestic Violence in the LGBTQ Community

I n many ways, the dynamics and issues related to intimate partner violence (IPV) in the lesbian, gay, bisexual, transgender, and queer/questioning (LGBTQ) community are the same as those in male-female intimate partner relationships, but in some ways, it is unique. With respect to the LGBTQ community, there are additional avenues of victimization: the fear of being outed by an abusive partner before being ready, and the fear of reprisal from an uneducated or biased system.

It is often incorrectly assumed that violence between a lesbian, bisexual, transgender, or gay couple must be mutual. The violence between such couples is often discussed as "just a cat fight" or "just a man-to-man" fight and not looked at, or treated, as the intimate partner violence it is. This perception is very different from that of male-female intimate partner violence. Same-sex and queer partners are still intimate partners, and laws against domestic violence fall under the same guidelines for all victims and offenders, regardless of their sexual orientation or lifestyle. Gay, lesbian, bisexual, transgender, and queer/questioning victims deserve the same treatment and response when calling for help as heterosexual victims would receive.

Many LGBTQ victims of domestic violence believe that in order to use existing services (such as a shelter, support group, or crisis hotline), they must lie about the nature of their intimate relationship. Asking for help or trying to leave an abusive relationship can mean coming out, which for many victims is a major life decision. A victim fearing that he or she would be forced out of the closet if asking for help may stay in an abusive relationship longer than is safe, giving further control to the abusive partner.

LGBTQ victims of domestic violence often fears additional victimization by the people and the system that are supposed to assist, support, and protect them. Often the largest obstacle to asking for or receiving help is the fear of re-victimization. Many LGBTQ victims fear that coming out to service providers who are not discreet with their information could lead to the loss of home, job, custody of children, etc. In addition, many LGBTQ victims fear that they will be judged and/or criticized by the person who is supposed to be supporting and helping them.

Leslie and Lee Ann

Leslie and Lee Ann are both twenty-two years old and seniors in college. They met their freshman year, and by April of the following year, they began a committed intimate partner relationship. Everyone thought they were BFFs (best friends forever). Only a select few close friends knew the truth about their relationship. Lee Ann comes from a very religious family and, as a result, is still in the closet, fearing that her family would disapprove of her and her relationship, perhaps even reject or disown her. They believe in "one man, one woman" relationships only and that anything else is perverse, deviant, and against God.

When Leslie begins to be abusive, telling Lee Ann that she is getting fat after gaining five pounds and that she is stupid after receiving a 68 percent on her calculus exam, Lee Ann feels she had no one to talk to. One day, after coming home from a math study group (because of her struggles with calculus), Lee Ann is surprised when Leslie grabs her, accusing her of having an affair. She shakes Lee Ann so hard that she leaves bruises on her arm. To make sure that Lee Ann doesn't leave, Leslie threatens to out her to her family, knowing that they would reject and perhaps even disown her if they knew.

Using sexual orientation and a partner's fear of being outed, although not illegal, is abuse.

Why Victims Stay—and Leave

A victim of domestic violence is beaten down long before she [or he] is ever beaten up.

—*Author unknown*

Contrary to the all-too-often overheard comments, victims don't stay or return to abusive or violent relationships because they are stupid or like being hit, hurt, or abused in any other way. Over the years, victims have shared with me why they have stayed and/or returned to abusive relationships. Below is a list of the most common reasons victims stayed or returned to abusive relationships.

Hope versus Fantasy

Victims of domestic violence often report that they stay (and/or return) to controlling and abusive partners because they keep hoping that the abusive partner will change. In cases of domestic violence, these victims are frequently confusing hope with fantasy. According to *Merriam-Webster's Online Dictionary*, the word *hope* is defined as "wanting something to happen or be true."[7] *Fantasy* is defined as "the faculty of imagining things that are impossible or improbable" (Merriam-Webster, 2017).

Why would the controlling or abusive partner change? He or she has all the control in the relationship and wants to keep it that way. Victims want to believe that their partners will change. This hope or fantasy is often fed into during the honeymoon stage, when the victim believes that the abusive partner will change. The abusive partner changing is highly improbable, as is the hope or fantasy that the controlling or abusive behaviors will end. On the contrary, the need to control, or behaviors related to being in control, usually tend to escalate, not end, over time.

In addition to the fantasy, the victim also fears that if he or she leaves, the abuser will change: "I suffered through all of this for nothing, and the new partner gets the good Jack (or Jane) after I did all the hard work? No way!"

Hope and Clancy

Hope loved Clancy and begged him to get help, but why should he? All his wants and needs were getting met. He was the one in control and was always getting his way. Clancy not only took no responsibility for his abusive behaviors, but also he had no motivation to change. Hope was afraid that if she left and he changed, then she would have had to endure all the bad stuff while the new girlfriend would get the good Clancy. She said, "That wouldn't be fair after all I've been through with him." She was going to stick it out, just in case.

Fanny and Frank

When Fanny met Frank, he was "charming, handsome, and so good," she said, "not only to me, but to my kids too!" As time went on and Fanny and Frank entered a committed relationship,

Frank became emotionally and mentally abusive and would often say to her, "You are a fat, ugly bitch. You can't do anything right. You are so lucky that I love you, because nobody else would ever want you." After every fight Frank would seem charming again, but it would only last a few days. Still, those few days fed into the fantasy that he was really sorry and would change. She would see the man she "fell in love with"—the man, or the facade, that he presented to her in order to hook her in. Fanny was in love with the fantasy of who she thought Frank was, not the Frank that she was actually in a relationship with. She was not willing to let go of the fantasy, and as a result, she was unable to let go of Frank.

Grief and Loss

When (or if) an abusive relationship ends, the victim often has to grieve both the loss of the relationship and the loss of the fantasy of what should have been or what could have been had her or his partner changed.

Greta and Gary
Greta and Gary had been living together for twelve years. Gary was a law enforcement officer who arrested Greta's ex-husband after he threw her against the wall so hard that he dislocated her shoulder. For the first eight months that Greta was with Gary she felt safe, special, and loved, but things changed. As time went on Gary's behavior became more controlling. He would tell her, "I just want to make sure you're safe." At first she believed him—or at least wanted to. She began to see that Gary's controlling behaviors looked more and more like her ex-husband's abusive behaviors, even though

Gary never hit her. He screamed, he yelled, he belittled, he accused her of having affairs, and he called her names, but she couldn't let go of the Gary she'd fallen in love with. She was sure that it was just the stress of his job and that once he retired he would go back to the sweet, caring, and loving Gary she'd met twelve years before.

She wasn't going to just walk away. After all the time she had invested and all the abuse she had endured, she wasn't going to allow some other woman to get the good Gary after he changed. She would stick it out.

Eventually Greta could no long tolerate the abuse and had to leave the relationship. Not only did Greta have to grieve the loss of the relationship but also the loss of what should have been.

Privacy versus Secrecy

Privacy and secrecy are similar, but they are *not* the same. Privacy refers to boundaries and personal space. For example, when most people go to the bathroom, they shut the door. They are not hiding anything. They just want their personal space and for it to be respected. Walking or barging in on a person in the bathroom with the door shut without knocking and without permission is a violation of that person's privacy. Secrecy goes beyond that. It's when a person is doing something immoral or illegal while in the bathroom and is afraid of getting caught or when the activity involves a sense of guilt and/or shame. Guilt is when you feel bad for what you have done. Shame is when you feel bad for who you are. Unlike privacy, secrecy involves shame and guilt and fear. Victims often stay in abusive relationships due to feelings of shame regarding the abuse (and/or past abuse). The toxicity of the secrecy, coupled with the victim's related feelings of shame and low to no self-esteem, contribute to his or her belief that "no one else would ever want me or treat me any better if they did."

Pedro and Petra
Petra and Pedro have been together for almost a year. Pedro adores Petra and has never cheated on her nor given her reason to believe that he has. Petra is very jealous and controlling and does not understand the difference between privacy and secrecy. She insists on constantly checking his phone and e-mail and often shows up at his place of employment at lunch to see what he is doing or who he is talking with. The more he asks that she respect his privacy, the more she is convinced that he is hiding something. Pedro understands and respects the need for privacy. He would never go into Petra's desk, nor would he ever go into her purse. Petra has a secret. She got fired from her job five weeks before for not being able to keep up. She applied for unemployment but is ashamed to tell Pedro was happened. All she keeps thinking is, *What would he think if he knew that I failed—that I am a failure?*

Learned Helplessness

Learned helplessness is akin to Stockholm syndrome. It occurs when a person has been isolated, controlled, and victimized over an extended period of time. She or he gets told that every decision she or he makes is wrong or stupid and that she or he is incompetent. The victim gets punished for each decision. Even when a victim makes a choice that she or he was told was correct a day or so prior, it is no longer viewed as correct. The victim comes to believe or learn that she or he is indeed too helpless or stupid to make the right decision. Eventually the victim becomes emotionally paralyzed and needs her or his partner (or another person) to make decisions for her or him. Learned helplessness is a form of brainwashing that the controlling and abusive partner uses in order to gain and maintain control, sending the message (and creating a perceived reality) that the only decisions, choices, and beliefs that matter are the abuser's own. This manipulation game is set up to ensure the victim can never win.

La Donna
La Donna has left a long-term abusive marriage and has made a decision to divorce her abusive and controlling husband. She only had $1,700 when she left. She has found an apartment in what she described as "a safe and affordable neighborhood." La Donna's soon-to-be ex-husband, Leroy, has now hired a so-called shark as a divorce attorney. Faced with this threat, La Donna fears if she doesn't hire someone good, she will be eaten alive. So she meets with a great attorney who is willing to take a fifteen-hundred-dollar retainer. La Donna doesn't know what to do. She is struggling with the decision between whether to use the limited amount of money she has for the first month's rent and security deposit on the apartment or to use it to hire the attorney. She is struggling with the idea that whatever decision she makes will be (or at least is highly likely to be) the wrong decision. The rental property La Donna has been considering becomes unavailable. The decision has now been made: she will use the money to hire the attorney. One choice is no longer an option, so La Donna has to go with the other by default, not really by choice.

Lack of Emotional Support from Family and/or Friends

Many people understand what emotional abuse is but don't understand the emotional (and psychological) impact of someone being isolated from friends, family, and other people who may be a source of support, encouragement, and/or empowerment.

Isolation and removing a victim from his or her support system are common manipulative and coercive tactics used by the controlling or abusive partner as soon as the victim is hooked into the relationship. Isolation takes away the victim's ability to recognize the abusive partner's behavior or take a reality check regarding his or her own sanity. Also, as time goes on, victims often stay because family and previous friends have withdrawn their support. This can happen when loved ones have helped the victim leave and then watched the victim return to the abusive partner. Family and previous friends may feel the victim chose the abusive partner over them and refuse to be betrayed again.

Alona and Alan

Alona was very close to her family. Throughout much of her life, her older sister was her best friend and her mother was her greatest source of comfort and support. In the beginning of Alona's relationship with Alan, neither of them trusted him. When Alona and Alan were dating, Alan hit her. Alona told her family that it was because he was drunk. They knew better and told her so. She told them that she loved him and that he promised it would never happen again, and she believed him. Two months after they got married, Alan told Alona that he wanted to move from Minnesota to Florida. He told her he wanted to get away from the cold and snow and start their life together "in a happy, warm place by the water." What he didn't tell her was that he wanted to move her away from her support system. She agreed. Within a year, she was living in Florida with no family, friends, or job—and with a baby. After they moved to Florida, away from Alona's support system, Alan became more and more abusive. Alona was too embarrassed to call home and talk about her problems with Alan. Her day-to-day life was spent at home with the baby. Alona began to feel alone. She no longer had anyone to talk to or depend on—except for Alan. Mission accomplished!

Fear of Being Punished or Even Killed for Leaving the Relationship

Research reports that 70 percent of women killed in abusive relationships are killed when (or shortly after) they leave (Lawson, 2005). When a victim leaves, she or he takes control back and away from the abusive partner. Victims do not stay because they like getting hit; they just fear that if they leave they will be hit harder or worse.

Patrick and Portia
Patrick seldom hit Portia; he generally controlled her in other ways. He knew that she was unhappy in the relationship and frequently told her, "I love you to death," "You are my everything," and "If I can't have you, nobody else will." Patrick had a lot of money, power, and influence. Portia wanted so badly to leave but was afraid of what Patrick would do. Portia was haunted by the memory of her best childhood friend, Katie, who had been in a similar situation. When Katie told her husband she wanted a divorce, he beat her so badly she ended up in the hospital. Katie told everyone (except Portia) that she was robbed in the parking lot at the mall. Portia was afraid that if she left, she would be next.

Feeling Responsible for the Abuse

Emotional and mental abuse, especially long term, are a form of brainwashing. A victim who is told that everything is his or her fault and that everything he or she says and does is wrong begins to believe it. As a result, the victim often takes responsibility for the abuse, believing that he or she caused it. The abusive partner seldom takes responsibility, except when he or she is sucking up during the honeymoon stage after a violent episode.

Florrie and Frank

"I am such a bad wife. I never do anything right! I always make Frank so mad. I don't work. My only jobs are taking care of Frank and the kids and keeping the house clean, and I can't even do that right! If only I did a better job cleaning the house and didn't make him so mad, then he wouldn't have to hit me." Florrie is not only taking responsibility for making Frank mad, but she is also taking responsibility for his violent actions.

Feelings of Guilt about the Failure of the Relationship and Breaking up the Family

Many victims believe that a relationship or marriage that ends is a failed relationship, and they blame themselves for the failure. Many believe that this failure makes them responsible for their children growing up in a so-called broken home. They want their children be able to grow up with both a mother and a father (or for gay and lesbian parents, both fathers or both mothers). Many parents also believe that if a child is not being abused, or if the intimate partner abuse occurs when the child is in the other room, sleeping, or not at home, then the child is not being negatively affected or harmed by the abuse.

Gilda and Gus

Gilda's parents divorced when she was six. She made a promise to herself that her children would *never* come from a broken home. She tries so hard to be a good wife so Gus will not have to get so angry and be so violent, but he keeps going off on her. Gilda believes that she has failed. She's failed as a wife and as a mother. If she leaves, she will have failed the marriage. All she'd had to do was take care of her husband the house and the children, and she couldn't even do that right.

The one thing she believes she is going to do right is make sure that her children grow up in an intact family—even an unhealthy and abusive home is better than a broken home. Or is it?

Financial Dependence

I have previously discussed financial control, a form of abuse that prevents one partner from having access to money or the ability to make financial decisions. In this section, we are discussing the anticipation or fear of what would happen should the victim leave. The victim questions whether or not she or he will have the resources to take care of herself or himself (and the children). This is an additional form of financial abuse. In abusive relationships, victims are frequently financially dependent on their partners. Part of the control is set up and maintained by the abusive partner, who controls the finances and/or financial accounts. The victim may have no or limited access to the accounts or may fear being punished if she or he tries to access or remove money from them. When a victim leaves the relationship, the financially controlling partner not only often removes access for bank accounts, but they also cancel credit cards, leaving the victim without access to any financial resources. Often credit cards are only initially left open to track the victim's whereabouts and behaviors, and then they too are canceled once the victims whereabouts has been established.

Denise and Daniel

Daniel and Denise had been together for six years. Denise was financially dependent on Daniel. They met in their sophomore year of college. At the beginning of their senior year, Denise got pregnant and was placed on bed rest due to medical complications. As a result, she had to take some time off from school.

Once the baby was born, one thing led to another, and she never went back. Denise and Daniel lived together but never married. Daniel got a great job, making over six figures, and promised to take care of her and the baby. She trusted and believed him. Daniel was always, according to Denise, "a little into himself," but as time went on he became more manipulative and controlling. He always needed to be right, win, and have his way. Daniel would punish Denise by withholding money and freezing her credit cards. He had the "I pay, I say" mentality and implemented it in every area of their relationship. Denise wondered how she would be able to support herself and her child without a college degree or any real job history. She felt trapped, so she stayed.

Fear of Losing Their Children

Abusive partners often tell their victims that if they leave the relationship, they will either "never see the children again" or the abusive partner will convince the judge that the victim is a terrible parent and mentally unstable, getting full custody of, as the abusive partner will put it, "*my* kids."

Even though most states now have joint custody laws and look at what is in the best interest of the child, victims are often so beaten down they feel powerless and voiceless in the relationship. They fear that their powerlessness will carry over into the courtroom. Often the victim believes that by being the object of the abuse, the victim is sheltering his or her children from potential risk. The fear that the abusive partner, with her or his win-at-all costs attitude, might be granted even partial custody that results in the non-abusive parent not being there to protect the children makes leaving and possible custody hearings dangerous.

As a result, the victim is not willing to take the chance. The victim stays in the relationship to insure being able to protect his or her children. After all, if the abusive partner gets custody (sometimes even partial custody), the victim fears for the children's safety because they will be there without the eyes, or perceived protection, of the non-abusive parent.

Faith and Lars
Faith and Lars have twin seven-year-old boys. Lars began to struggle with anxiety and depression eight months into the abusive relationship with Faith. Lars is employed as a bookkeeper and often works from home. It is important to him that he is there when the boys get home from school. Unhappy in the relationship, Lars always tells Faith, "My children are my life. I would do anything for them," and he means it. Faith is a cardiac surgeon at the local hospital. Although Faith has never hit him (after all, she's too smart to risk criminal charges that could put her medical license at risk), she is controlling and manipulative and always puts him down, calls him names, and threatens him. The one time Lars mentioned divorce, Faith responded by saying, "If you try to leave me, I will spend every dollar I have to make sure that I get full custody of the boys. I will hire the best lawyers and have them tell the court that you are mentally unstable and take medication for your mental health issues." Whenever she thought Lars was thinking about the possibility of leaving her, Faith would threaten, "I will out-lawyer you, I will outspend you, and I will win! So, unless you want to lose your kids, don't even *think* about it!" Even though the law in his state favored 50/50 parental time sharing, Lars feared losing complete custody of his children, so he stayed.

Lack of Faith and Trust in Law Enforcement

When discussing past incidence of domestic violence, victims often mistakenly say, "When I got him [or her] arrested for hitting me ..." Victims don't get their partners arrested. The abusive partners' illegal, battering behaviors get them arrested. Victims often take responsibility not only for the abuse but for the arrest as well. The abusive partner often blames and punishes the victim for calling law enforcement, speaking with law enforcement, or getting the abusive partner locked up. Even with an injunction for protection (restraining order), a victim knows in reality that there is only so much law enforcement can do to keep the victim (and the victim's children) safe. Even if she or he is arrested, the battering partner will likely be out the following day, putting the victim at risk for being punished once again.

Lovey and Leroy
Lovey was so afraid of Leroy, but she knew if she called the police he would be out in a day and then punish her for getting him locked up. The previous year, when Leroy was arrested for domestic violence, he got out the next day and nearly broke her arm. He told her he had to teach her lesson to make sure she didn't try that again. She didn't believe that the police could protect her or her children. On the contrary, she knew the police would only make it worse! Lovey is not alone in believing that calling law enforcement (911) is not an option. Many victims of domestic violence fear reprisal from their abusive partners' arrests. Lovey believed that even if calling 911 made things safer temporarily, in the long run it would likely make them much worse. Leroy blamed her when the neighbor called. He told her that it was her fault because she "screamed too loud" when he hit her. No matter who calls law enforcement, Lovey often takes the blame.

Feelings of So-Called Love

The term *unconditional love* is often used when someone loves another but doesn't like the other's behaviors. Often victims don't know or aren't ready to accept that loving someone doesn't mean being forced to accept abusive or other unacceptable behavior. Victims also struggle with the concept of loving their partners from someplace else. The belief is that when you love someone, you stay with him or her.

Louis and Lois
Louis loved Lois. He told everyone that when they met and fell in love she was the most beautiful, smartest, and most loving woman he had ever known. Two years later, in spite of the fact that she had begun to control and micromanage him, he was still in love. If she wasn't calling, she was texting to ask what he was doing, who he was talking to, and when he would be home, etc., but Louis didn't tell that to anyone—partly because he was embarrassed and partly because he needed to keep the fantasy alive.
He loved her with all his heart, even though she'd broken his heart when she'd had an affair with someone she'd met online the previous year. He just kept saying that he loved her. But was he in love with her or in love with the idea of being in love? Perhaps he was in love with the romantic memories of the way things were when the relationship first started.
Regardless, Louis was stuck in an abusive relationship, waiting for the Lois he'd first fallen in love with.

Lack of Faith and Trust in the Court System

Victims who don't have a voice in their relationships fear that they won't have a voice in court. The court system is more and more referred to as the *legal* system rather than the *justice* system. There is a great deal of inconsistency and injustice in the legal system. In court, the truth is driven by data and is based only on what can be proven, not on what is or what may be true. Attorneys often have true information thrown out or disregarded because of a technicality or a lack of "sufficient evidence." Victims who already feel powerless often fear a system that will be swayed by their partners, who will portray them as emotionally unstable, lazy, and/or unfit to care for the children. Sadly, because of the fear that their partners are using the legal system to re-victimize them, victims often do come across as overly emotional (especially if they fear losing their children) and appear to reinforce the allegations of emotional instability made by their abusive partners.

Autumn and Anthony

Autumn and Anthony had been married seventeen years. They had three children, two dogs, a cat, and a fish. She wanted to leave him, to go somewhere safe with her children and start over. But she was afraid. Florida was a 50/50 joint parenting state. She was afraid of what would happen if the court ordered the children to go with their father 50 percent of the time and she wouldn't be there to take care of them or to protect them. She had seen it with so many of her friends. Their exes wouldn't even let them talk to the kids on the cell phone on the days or nights the court gave them. They referred to it as "my time," as though allowing the children access to the other parent would somehow give that parent something that belonged to them. Perhaps they just wanted to punish the other parent over and over for leaving—by using the children.

Religious Reasons

Very often victims who have strong religious beliefs will stay in abusive relationships, especially those who are married, because, according to some victims, "the church does not believe in divorce" or "I said a vow before God, so I can't leave." Often religious partners will bogusly but effectively use Bible verses to justify their behaviors and manipulate their partners. For some religious victims, public image in the religious community and in front of its leaders is often placed above personal happiness and safety.

Rene and Radford
Ten years ago Rene vowed before God to "love, honor, and cherish Radford, 'til death do us part." She now desperately wants to leave him but says, "It would be against God and the church to break my vows and get a divorce. I will just pray that God will help me get through this." Rene stays, prays, and emotionally slips away.

Why Victims Leave

Many victims stay because of their children, but that is also one of the biggest reasons they leave. They may fear losing the children to the state for "failure to protect," or they may just finally realize that no matter what they do, the abuse is not going to end and is likely to escalate. The victim comes to the point of saying, "I can't take it anymore," creates a safety plan, and finally leaves—never to return.

Vivian and Larry

Vivian and Larry have been together off and on for six years. They have been married five years and have three children: four-year-old twins Conrad and Connie and three-year-old Callie. Viv has left Larry twice—once before they got married and once after, but she returned both times because she loved him and wanted to make sure that she did everything she could to keep her family together.

One night when Viv and Larry were fighting, Larry began trying to make her understand the importance of not "excessively and carelessly spending money." Vivian had bought new sheets, bedspreads, and paint so she could redo the twins' bedroom, because it still looked more like a nursery than a child's room. Conrad walked in and saw his father yelling and threatening and hitting his mother. Conrad screamed and yelled, "Stop hurting Mommy!" Larry told Conrad, "Mommy and I are just having a conversation, and I lost my temper. I would never hurt Mommy or any of you kids. You know I love you all." At the moment, Vivian realized Larry not only would hurt her (as he had been doing), but even worse, Larry could hurt her children.

Although Larry had isolated his wife from her immediate family, Vivian called her mother, who she hadn't spoken to in two years, and asked for help. Within a month, Vivian created and implemented a safety plan, moved out, and filed for divorce.

John and Joan

John and Joan have been married seven years and have two children, six-year-old Kalie and four-year-old Kyle. Joan is very abusive to and controlling of John. John is afraid to make Joan mad because she always finds non-physical ways to punish him. She frequently accuses him of trying to make the children like him better by reading them a story or playing with them in the yard. Joan threatens that if John tries to leave, she will lie and accuse him of being abusive to her and get a restraining order because she is afraid. During the last year of their marriage, John notices that Joan is not only controlling and abusive with him, but she puts him down, punishes him, and undermines his parental authority in front of the children. His children begin to ask him questions about "what Mommy said" about him, but John doesn't want to speak ill of their mother. In response to Joan telling the children that John would rather be at work than home with them, John assures the children that he would prefer to be with them but has to work to support the family. Hurting and controlling him was one thing, but John is not going to let Joan poison his children against him. He decides to call a lawyer, make an appointment, and file for a divorce.

Kenny and Karen

Kenny and Karin have been together two years and have a son named Bobbie, who is eight months old. Kenny recently went to shoot some pool and have a few beers after work and then came home drunk and wanting sex. Karin was not in the mood. When she said no, he got angry and violent. The baby was sleeping in his crib in another room when the incident occurred. Kenny was screaming at Karin so loud that a neighbor called the police.

When the police arrived, they arrested Kenny (who would be released from jail the next morning) and called the child abuse hotline. The investigator from child services told Karin if she didn't "leave and stay away from Kenny" they would remove the baby for "failure to protect." Karin didn't want to leave but wasn't going to risk losing her baby, so she did what they said. Karin left Kenny and filed for a restraining order as they insisted. This made Kenny angry, and he violated it three times before he was rearrested and finally left her alone.

Leaving an abusive relationship is difficult, especially with children. Victims are often surprised to find that the amount of strength, endurance, and perseverance it takes to stay in an abusive relationship is more than what it takes to leave. You are not alone. If you want to leave an abusive relationship and feel that you can't or don't know how, help is available. If family and/or friends aren't an option for you, there are hotlines, shelters, and a number of social service agencies that can and will help.

Trauma and Domestic Violence

According to the Substance Abuse and Mental Health Agency (SAMHSA) "Individual trauma results from an event, series of events, or set of circumstances that is experienced by an individual as physically or emotionally harmful or life threatening and that has lasting adverse effects on the individual's functioning and mental, physical, social, emotional, or spiritual well-being." (SAMHSA 2014). The word "trauma" means "wound" in Greek Originally, it was just used for physical injuries but now is used for emotional injuries as well (Merriam-Webster, 2017).

Trauma is often the overwhelming amount of stress that exceeds one's ability to cope or integrate the emotions involved with that experience. It is not the event itself that determines whether or not it will be a traumatic experience but how the person experiences and perceives the event.

Traumatizing events (car accidents, natural disasters, bad breakups, witnessing horrific events, etc.) can be traumatic even when there is no physical harm or damage. I remember reading a newspaper article about a father who murdered the mother and left the two-year-old son alone in the house with his dead mother. When the reporter wrote about the child, he said, "The child was unharmed." Even though the child endured no physical harm, the emotional, mental, and spiritual harm would have been significant. In addition to having lost both of his parents, at some point in his life the child will have to deal with the fact that his father was the one who killed his mother. Just because there was no physical harm certainly does not mean that this young boy was not traumatized and significantly harmed.

Beginning in the late 1980s and early 1990s, researchers began to recognize and affirm a clinical link between intimate partner violence and post-traumatic stress disorder (PTSD). Unlike trauma victims of war or onetime victims of rape by a stranger, victims of domestic violence often report higher levels of violence or exposure to violence as well as trauma-related symptoms (Astin, Lawrence, and Foy, 1993, p. 26).

Victims of intimate partner violence often exhibit trauma-related symptoms because they are often victimized and traumatized repeatedly over an extended period of time. In addition, when the violence is perpetrated by someone whom the victim loves, trusts, and often has had children with the impact of the trauma is that much more severe.

PTSD is not only a result of the physical, emotional, psychological, and/or sexual violence that a victim of domestic violence has already experienced in the relationship, but it is also the result of the partner's controlling, manipulative, and isolating actions causing continued fear for one's safety.

Victims of domestic violence are often not going to tell others what is going on. If they can't trust the person they love, the one who is supposed to love and protect them, why should they trust anyone else? Just because a person doesn't tell anyone that he or she is being abused does not mean that it isn't happening. In fact, the more violent the abuse, the bigger the fear, and the less likely the victim will tell anyone. Also, the greater the self-blame, the greater the shame, and the less likely the victim is to share his or her secret that he or she is being abused.

Part 1: Three Components of Trauma (or Traumatic Events)

Life is filled with stressful and uncomfortable events and experiences, but that does not mean they are traumatic. In order for the event to be categorized as traumatic, it must have three basic components:

(1) The event (person) causing the trauma was *unexpected* and *overwhelming*.
(2) The person was *not prepared* for the event or trauma.
(3) The person felt *helpless in stopping the event* from happening.

Part 2: Three Types of Trauma

There are basically three different types of trauma: trauma caused by nature, trauma caused by accident, and trauma caused by a person.

Traumas Caused by Nature

Traumas caused by nature, such as hurricanes, volcanoes, tornados, or floods, often find people either mad at God ("I can't believe he would let this happen to me") or not believing in God ("If there really were a God, he never would have allowed this to happen to me"). Traumas caused by nature seldom cause feelings of self-blame or shame, and victims of the trauma often have the support of family, friends, other members of the community, and beyond.

Nancy and Nathan
Nancy and Nathan survived Hurricane Katrina, a horrific trauma caused by nature. Although they were petrified during the hurricane, as soon as it was over everyone in their neighborhood banned together and began supporting and helping each other.

Friends and family called and offered encouragement, support, and even some financial assistance. Nathan had been raised in a very religious family and believed in God, but after the hurricane he began to wonder if God really existed. He kept asking, "If God really existed, he wouldn't let this happen to me and my family, would he?" Nancy, on the other hand, continues to believe in God but says she is "angry with him for letting this happen to me and my family."

Traumas Caused by Accident

Unintentional human-caused traumas are caused by accident or without intention of harm, such as auto accidents, falling or rolling off a roof, etc. Unlike traumas experienced by victims of domestic or sexual violence, traumas caused by accident may or may not include self-blame by the person experiencing the trauma.

Andy and Andria
Andy loved Christmas. It was his favorite holiday of the year, and he loved putting up lights. One Christmas he was trying to balance Santa's sleigh on the roof when he fell off! He broke his hip and right leg but thankfully did not hurt his neck or back. His wife, Andria, watched him fall through the kitchen window. She immediately dropped the dish she was washing, called 911, and went to see if he was okay.

Traumas Caused by Another Person

With traumas intentionally caused by another person (such as domestic or sexual violence, child abuse or incest, war, criminal activity or violence, etc.), the dynamic is often much different. The trauma and victimization is usually caused by a person the victim loves and trusts. The element of betrayal often magnifies the emotional and psychological impact of the trauma when the person who is supposed to love and protect the victim is the person violating him or her. Unlike other types of trauma, traumas intentionally caused by another person often result in self-blame and shame, with no safe person or place to turn to.

There is also often an element of self-blame and shame unique to victims of domestic and/or sexual violence. Judgment and blame by others are also much more common with victims of domestic and sexual violence, as evidenced by comments like, "If she doesn't like it, why doesn't she just leave? If someone hit me, I'd be gone in a minute." People who make such comments don't understand that victims are beaten down many times before they are ever beaten up.

Victims of sexual assault are often blamed for the assault, when the blame should be on the perpetrator. Accusatory statements like, "She was drunk or high" and "Did you see what she was wearing?" put the blame on the wrong person.

Trauma caused by a stranger, acquaintance, coworker, or other non-intimate friend or family member, although still traumatic, would likely have a lesser impact on the victim's feelings of self-blame, shame, resentment, and his or her support system.

Manny and Maria
Manny battered Maria. He bruised her cheek and broke her arm in three places. All her family is in Michigan. He is the only family she has here. They have two daughters, Mykayla (eleven) and Madison (seven). Manny was Maria's first love and the father of her children, and she is terrified to stay with him and even more terrified to leave him. He has threatened to kill her if she tries to leave. She believes him. She blames herself for not leaving years ago, when she had the chance, and for loving someone who can be so mean.

Part 3: Symptoms of Trauma

Symptoms of trauma are normal responses that often follow an abnormal (traumatic) event. These normal symptoms often further traumatize survivors, making them feel crazy—even though it's the trauma that's the problem, not them. Just because they feel crazy doesn't mean that they are. Not everyone who experiences a trauma meets the diagnostic criteria for PTSD, but most have trauma-related symptoms after the event. Victims of domestic or sexual violence and child abuse or neglect don't just survive an individual event; they survive an ongoing event or relationship with those who are supposed to love and protect them but who instead use their power to make traumatic impacts. Perpetrators of domestic violence will use this feeling of being crazy against victims, further intimidating, blaming, and shaming victims to maintain control and ensure that victims doesn't leave the relationship.

Physical Symptoms of Trauma

Some of the symptoms of trauma are physical.

Sleep disturbances (sleeping more or less than usual) and/or nightmares are one example. These types of sleep disturbance are not the same as generalized insomnia.

Sylvia and Sven
Sylvia can't sleep because she has nightmares about Sven throwing her up against the wall and telling her, "If you even try to leave me again and take my son, I'm gonna kill you." Sylvia also dreams about him kidnapping their son and taking him back to Sweden. The only time she gets a good, solid sleep is when she naps during the day while Sven is at work.

Significant decrease or increase in appetite is another physical symptom of trauma. Generally anxiety causes an increase in appetite and depression causes a decrease, but it varies from person to person.

Alice and Alva

Alva is six years old, and his sister, Alice, is eleven. Their mother recently married Andrew, who now is their stepfather. As soon as the honeymoon was over, so to speak, Andrew began sexually abusing them both. Alva is now so anxious that his stepfather will come back into his room and make him touch that "thing" to him again that he can't stop eating. His sister Alice is struggling with depression and as a result has no desire to eat. Since the abuse started six months ago, she has lost seven pounds, and people are starting to wonder if she is ill. Andrew has threatened to kill their mother and have them sent to a foster home if they tell, so they are afraid and are keeping their secret to themselves.

Lack of sex drive or impotence can also result from trauma. This goes well beyond an occasional "headache," the inability to "stand on demand," or other types of sexual dysfunction.

Lucy and Larry

Larry has never hit Lucy, but he is controlling and emotionally and mentally abusive to her. Larry complains that Lucy is never in the mood for sex. Lucy wishes he would understand that always being told what a "fat, ugly, worthless piece of shit" she is does nothing to make her feel like making love or even just having sex with him. Larry now adds "frigid" and "useless" to the names he calls her. Recently, Larry began to threaten, "If you won't have sex with me, I'll find someone else who will!"

Lack of energy is often misperceived by others to be laziness. It is not. A person uses so much energy to deal with the trauma that he or she has little, if any, energy left over for anything or anyone else. Sadly, this often includes the person's children.

Emma and Evan
Emma has been a victim of abuse all her life. She grew up in a violent home, left, and has now recreated that same environment in her new home with her boyfriend, Evan. Like her mother, Emma seldom gets out of bed—or wants to, anyway. As much as she loves her nine-month-old son, Elliott, when he cries in the middle of the night, she has to push herself to get up and go to his room to give him a bottle. She wants to get up but often doesn't have the energy. She finally just moved the baby's crib into her room so she wouldn't have to go so far. Evan comes home drunk and angry every day and punishes her for "being a lazy ass bitch." Emma is not lazy; she feels helpless and hopeless and is depressed.

Chronic and often unexplained pain also results from trauma. The pain is real, but the cause is a mystery. Medical professionals say everything looks good and that there are no signs of physical ailment, but the pain continues.

Charlene
Charlene was sexually abused throughout her childhood and at age twenty-eight is in an abusive relationship with her boss (who is twenty years older than she is). Charlene is thin and looks to be in good shape, but she frequently complains about severe body aches and chronic pain. Charlene's pain is real, but medically there is no explanation. She is often treated as though she were an addict seeking pain medication or as though she were a hypochondriac.

Not all the symptoms of trauma are physical.

Emotional Symptoms of Trauma

It is normal to be and feel emotional after a trauma. Some symptoms last longer than others, but generally just because someone is emotional after a trauma does not mean that the person has lost it, gone crazy, or stopped functioning. Nor does it mean that the person is unstable, irrational, or unable to care for himself or herself or others.

Depression is different from sadness and is accompanied by specific symptoms, such as frequent and spontaneous crying spells, the inability to shut one's thoughts off, and feelings of hopelessness and/or helplessness. Sadness is an emotion, while depression is a state of being in which a person feels a strong sense of dread and feels helpless and hopeless that his or her situation will change. A person does not have to be or feel suicidal to be depressed. A person who was helpless in stopping a trauma from happening often feels powerless to prevent it from happening again. The person feels as though he or she will never heal from the damage caused by the trauma.

Dena
Dena is not just sad; she's traumatized and depressed. She could not stop her stepfather from sexually abusing her from the time she was seven until she was twelve and her mother announced they were getting a divorce. When she was fourteen, her first boyfriend was abusive, and so was every boyfriend thereafter. Abuse may not be healthy, but for Dena, abuse is all she ever has known or believed she deserves. She doesn't believe that there are any other types of relationships. They all are or will be abusive—at least for her.

Feelings of anxiety also can result from trauma. Anxiety is different from stress and is sometimes accompanied by panic attacks. Feeling anxiety is part of the human experience, but debilitating anxiety and panic attacks often come from a place of deep fear and past or ongoing trauma; such anxiety or panic is often triggered by a smell, sound, item, event, or person.

Paula and Paul

Paula struggles with anxiety. She is always waiting for the other shoe to drop or overthinking what she did or didn't do that day, week, or other time period. Compounding her anxiety is her relationship with her partner, Paul, who Paula says has an "anger management problem." She believes it's her job to make sure that she doesn't make Paul angry.

Seemingly out of nowhere, Paula will sometimes begin to have trouble breathing and then begin to stutter. Soon she goes into a full-blown panic attack. Only later does Paula realize that her panic attack was not from "out of nowhere" but was likely triggered by a song on Pandora that had been playing when her first boyfriend sexually abused and raped her at the junior prom.

Feeling broken or damaged can also be a symptom of trauma. *Broken* and *damaged* are adjectives often used by victims of sexual assault, abuse, and rape. Sexual violence violates the soul and the spirit—not only the body. Victims of sexual trauma often seek out clinical professionals, believing they are broken and need to be fixed. In reality, they don't need to be fixed; they need to heal.

Betty and Bob

Betty's father and oldest brother sexually abused her as a child. She was also violently beaten and raped by Bob, her boyfriend and former so-called hero (he was the one who rescued her from her abusive family). Betty feels that she is broken and is damaged goods and that no one would ever want her. Betty has been tragically traumatized and is hurting and needs to heal.

Feelings of fearfulness are also symptoms of trauma. Being fearful or afraid is different from being paranoid. A person who is afraid that something bad will happen, especially after it already has, perhaps more than once, is not paranoid; he or she is simply afraid. Just because a person may not reveal the true basis of his or her fear to someone, especially a shame-based fear, does not mean that it does not exist or have merit.

Francine and Fred

Throughout her childhood, Francine watched her father beat her mother. Furthermore, a family friend sexually abused her from ages seven through eleven, and her first boyfriend, Fred, told her that he would kill her if she ever tried to leave him. Eight months later she couldn't take it anymore and left anyway. Fred has been stalking Francine for two months (since the day she left). She is not paranoid; she is scared!

Displaying obsessive and/or compulsive behaviors can also be a symptom of trauma. Trauma causes feelings of helplessness and chaos. Obsessive or compulsive behaviors often are coping mechanisms meant to turn chaos into order. They are also attempts to give a person a feeling of control over his or her life or situation.

Olivia and Oliver
Olivia's friends always say, "Olivia is the most organized person I have ever seen. Even her lists have lists." Olivia won't leave anything to chance. She organizes and controls everything in her life, except her relationship (where she feels she has no control). Oliver has never hit her—nor would he—but he makes all the decisions, always has to be right, and always has to have the last word. Olivia feels that she is allowed no control and no voice and that is helpless in her relationship. She compensates by controlling her environment and all other aspects of her life.

Emotional numbness and guardedness can also accompany trauma. A person who has been badly hurt and/or traumatized often puts an emotional wall up to try to prevent or minimize further hurt or violation. This wall is not about personality, ego, or social status; it's about emotional safety and, for some, perhaps even survival. Having an emotional wall psychologically enables people who have been previously hurt or traumatized to protect themselves from letting someone in or becoming vulnerable to being hurt, violated, or abandoned again.

Nancy and Ned
Nancy's biological father left before she was born, and two of her three stepfathers sexually abused her. Nancy's mother ignored and neglected her, and Nancy's ex-husband, Ned, beat her. Trusting anyone (except her dog Tripod, who was born with only three legs) or allowing herself to be vulnerable are not options. The Great Wall of China is more flexible than she. Anytime someone brings up the idea of her getting involved in another relationship, she says, "Never again. I am not going to let anyone get close to me ever again!"

Learned helplessness and having no control over one's life, actions, and/or reactions may also be symptoms of past trauma. Often victims stay in abusive relationships because they believe they cannot do anything right and need their partners to help make good decisions. They have been told for so long that every decision they make is wrong, so they refuse to make decisions on their own. They are afraid they will make the wrong one again and either get punished for the decision or make their partners become disappointed or upset. Over time, they become brainwashed to believe they are incapable of making appropriate decisions.

Holly

Holly spent her childhood being told that nothing she did was right or good enough. Every partner she has ever had has told her the same thing. As a result, Holly believes that it must be true. Her self-esteem is minimal, and she feels that whatever decision she makes will be wrong or will be overridden by someone else with more power (such as a parent, a partner, or a boss).

When needing to do a task, Holly often asks herself, "Why bother?" This makes her seem lazy, but in reality she is just feeling lost, overwhelmed, and defeated.

Withdrawal from relationships and routines can also be a symptom of trauma. This withdrawal could be from trauma-related triggers, such as an intimate partner trying to isolate his or her partner. Withdrawal from relationships and routines is also a symptom of depression and addiction. This is a big red flag! Pay attention. If someone you love or care about is no longer showing up to classes, functions, or events or is not returning calls, texts, and/ or e-mails, you may want to check in with that person and find out what's going on.

Wendy
Wendy loved to windsurf. She and her old college roommate would go down to the beach and windsurf two to three times a month—that is, until she was attacked at the beach. Now Wendy has not only stopped windsurfing, but she also doesn't go to the beach anymore. In addition, she has stopped answering her phone, and she doesn't respond to text messages or posts on any social media.

Irritability, anger, and/or resentfulness of others might also be symptoms of trauma. If the trauma is the result of a violation, of course the victim is going to be angry, especially if the violation was enacted by someone he or she loved or cared about and trusted! This anger and/or resentment is not reserved for the perpetrator alone. The victim may also be resentful and blame others who know or knew about the violation and did nothing to help stop it. The victim might also be angry at those who do not acknowledge a violation occurred and/or do not validate the victim's feelings about the trauma.

Perpetrators often act one way toward the victim and a totally different way toward others in public (like Dr. Jekyll/Mr. Hyde). This too often makes the victim resentful, because he or she is being violated and/or traumatized, and nobody gets it. Other people are fooled by the show the abuser puts on in order to manipulate others' perceptions of his or her personality and behaviors.

Irene
Irene is angry. She has been victimized behind closed doors all her life—first by three of her mother's boyfriends, and now by her husband. People often wondered how, or even if, Irene could be a victim. Not only is she neither meek nor quiet; she's always irritable and angry.

> People often mistake her anger and strong personality to mean that she couldn't be a victim in any situation. This belief is untrue; it is not only an inaccurate judgment of the victim but also a misperception of the reality of the situation.

Feelings of being stuck, trapped, and/or boxed in can also by symptoms of trauma. A child being abused by his or her parents and feeling afraid to tell because of the possible consequences often feels trapped or boxed in. A partner in a relationship will feel trapped after being told, "If I can't have you, nobody will," or, "If you leave me, I will make sure you lose custody of the children and never see them again." Although these threats may not be true, the victim believes them to be and creates his or her reality accordingly.

Steve and Stacey

Steve is a stay-at-home father. His wife, Stacey, is a successful businesswoman who controls all the finances as well as everything and everyone in the household. On one occasion, she threatened Steve with a knife, and on another, she tried to run him over with the car. Steve fears that if he were to tell anyone what is happening in his relationship with Stacey, no one would ever believe him. He is at least twice her size. She is a smooth talker and says that if he were to tell others, she would claim that he was the initial aggressor and that she was only fighting back. Steve wants to leave, but he feels trapped and stuck.

Behavioral Symptoms of Trauma

No one has the right to judge a victim's behaviors. Behaviors are not *good* or *bad*—those are judgment words. Behaviors are, however, either healthy or unhealthy, safe or unsafe, and/or legal or illegal. People who have experienced a traumatic event or relationship often engage in unhealthy, unsafe, and sometimes even illegal behaviors. Many of their behaviors have a positive intent, even if the behavior itself is not so positive.

Alcohol and/or substance abuse, also known as self-medicating, can be a behavioral symptom of trauma. Victims of trauma often try to medicate the pain themselves, which all too often leads to another whole set of unhealthy behaviors and related effects.

Alec
Alec couldn't deal with all the nightmares and flashbacks from his childhood abuse. He began drinking to relax. Before long, he added Xanax to deal with his stress. The amount and combinations of alcohol, Xanax, and other substances that he use, began to create more problems for Alec. He was arrested for driving under the influence and ended up in a court-ordered substance abuse treatment program.

Self-mutilating behaviors can also follow trauma. When a person is victimized by someone—especially an intimate partner, friend, or family member—the victim may feel as though she or he has no control. When self-mutilating, the victim can control when the pain starts and when it stops.

In some cases, in order to cope with the abuse, victims will shut down and become numb. Self-mutilation is a way to feel again. To them, feeling something, even pain, is better than feeling nothing.

Besides the sense of control and the feeling of release a victim may get from the cutting, many victims report that they want the pain on the outside to reflect the pain they feel on the inside. Self-mutilation is the antithesis of control and therefore an unhealthy and unsafe antidote to trauma.

Sophie and Summer

Sophie and Summer had been victims of incest. Because of this, Sophie was sick and tired of everyone else controlling her life, including her teachers, her bosses, and now her boyfriend. They were always hurting her, and she couldn't stop or control it. She was so shut down. She felt numb.

Sometimes she felt so dead inside that she wanted to hurt herself just to see if she was still alive. Sophie's sister Summer also cut herself but for a different reason. She felt that everyone else had control over her and her pain, but when she cut, she was in control—of when the pain started and, more importantly, when it ended. She believed that when she cut was the only time she had the control to make the pain stop. To Summer, that feeling of pain and her feeling of having control over it was exhilarating and addicting.

Eating disorders can be another behavioral symptom of trauma. Often a person who feels he or she has no control over his or her life or outer body will try to control what he or she eats, thereby controlling his or her inner body. Emotional eating, bingeing and purging, or starving oneself are often trauma-related responses and behaviors.

Betty and Bernie

Betty was nine years old when Bernie, who always asked Betty to call him her uncle, began sexually abusing her. "Uncle Bernie" would force Betty to put his penis into her mouth. By the time she was eleven (when he was still abusing her), she would put her finger down her throat every time she ate in order to try to purge the feeling of something being in her mouth. Her brother Billy, who was also being sexually abused by

Bernie, became an emotional eater. Unlike Betty, Billy never purged, but he also used food to self-medicate his pain and try to fill the void of emptiness that he felt. Billy's body weight, which was referred to as "morbidly obese" in his medical chart, was a metaphor for the weight of his emotional pain and trauma.

Compulsive behaviors can also be behavioral symptoms of trauma. Frequently a person who has experienced trauma feels helpless, as if he or she has no control over his or her life. As a result, such victims often engage in compulsive behaviors, not necessarily because they have obsessive compulsive disorder (OCD), but because they are trying to make order out of chaos and to create some type of structure to make them feel more in control of their lives and/or environments.

Olivia

Since Olivia was seven, a number of male figures in her life have sexually violated her. Olivia is now forty-two. She is involved in her third abusive marriage and has four children. She feels as if she has never had control over her body or her life, so she has tried to control her environment by keeping things neat and tidy. Olivia's appliances are so clean and shiny that her sister once used the toaster as a mirror to fix her makeup prior to leaving Olivia's house for a family dinner.

Hypervigilance can also be a symptom of trauma.

Harriett and Homer
Harriett is always "so on edge," as her friends used to say, "she would make coffee nervous." Harriet is always looking over her shoulder and jumps every time a window opens or door closes. When people first meet Harriett, they think she is paranoid. They don't understand that Harriett has spent her life in survival mode. She grew up in a violent home and is now living in a violent relationship with her boyfriend, Homer. Harriett goes through each day and night waiting for the proverbial shoe to drop.

Uncontrolled thoughts and flashbacks are also common symptoms of past or ongoing trauma. Flashbacks are small flashes of memories of a past trauma that appear without warning. These memories are often reported as flashing before the eyes from out of nowhere, often making the survivor of the trauma feel as if he or she is going crazy. In addition, these memories feel more like audio and/ or visual hallucinations because they seem so real. These trauma symptoms also often contribute to the trauma survivors' fear of being or going crazy.

Frequent engagement in unhealthy behaviors and/or choices can also by symptoms of trauma. People living in survival mode do not always make healthy choices. Their choices must be looked at as healthy or unhealthy, safe or unsafe, and/or legal or illegal— not judged as *good* or *bad* or *right* or *wrong*. People often judge another person's bad behaviors without understanding the victim's situation. When victims are living in survival mode, they are often reacting out of fear, pain, and feelings of helplessness. They need to be treated with kindness and understanding rather than be judged.

Ursala and Randy
Ursala was afraid of Randy and his rages. She was afraid to be awake and to go to sleep. She could not stop her brain from going over memories from Randy's violent outbursts. Ursala also would obsess about what would or could happen to her the next time Randy went off. When Ursala did finally fall asleep at night, she would often be awakened by her nightmares of Randy's violent rages. Ursala began drinking just to be able to sleep. First, it was occasionally, then frequently, and eventually every night. In time, Ursula became addicted to alcohol. When alcohol was unavailable, she often took other drugs—both over the counter and off the street. Ursala felt that everyone judged her, just as she judged herself. She would often say, "Maybe Randy is right. I am nothing more than a worthless piece-of-shit alcoholic and junkie."

Loss of belief in fairness and safety can also be a symptom of trauma. Before a trauma, people often believe that life is mostly fair. They believe they have control over their lives and outcomes, saying, "If I'm good, work hard, and do all the right things, only good things and success will happen to me." Trauma victimization removes those beliefs and takes away, or at least minimizes, a victim's feelings of safety and control over her or his life.

Shutting down altogether can be another symptom of trauma.

Salim
Salim was sexually abused by his grandfather from the time he was five until he was eleven, by an adult female babysitter when he was seven, and by another babysitter when he was nine. As a child, Salim's father beat him for not respecting his elders. He was abused, threatened, and beaten throughout his childhood, so Salim made the following decision at a young age:

"It is too painful to function in this world, so I'm just going to withdraw into myself where it's safer, I'm less vulnerable, and I won't really have to function anymore." As an adult, Salim suffers from major depression as well as severe anxiety and intimacy issues. Salim is not crazy; he's traumatized!

Cognitive Symptoms of Trauma

Trauma often affects a person's thoughts, their ability to concentrate or focus, and their memory.

Blocks in memory (especially as the memory relates to the trauma) are an example of a cognitive symptom of trauma. There is an old adage that says, "God never gives us more than we can handle." Perhaps that's why a victim does not or cannot remember any or all of the details of a trauma after it happens. The mind either hides the details or only reveals the details slowly to allow the victim to process the trauma in her or his own time. All too often, victims of domestic and/or sexual violence are accused of lying because they can't recall details or they change the details as the mind imparts the information. In spite of these inconsistencies (in most cases) victims are not lying; rather, they have either blocked the trauma, or details that were previously hidden slowly come to the surface.

Barbara and Ben
Barbara's friend left the club with a guy she met on the dance floor, leaving Barbara without a ride home.   Barbara ran into Ben, who was in her chemistry class at the university, and he offered her a ride. She accepted. Instead of taking her home, Ben brought her to an empty lot and raped her. When she called the police, they began asking questions, but Barbara couldn't remember what Ben was wearing, what kind of car he was driving, or where they had gone together.

> As the days went on, Barbara began to remember bits and pieces of the rape, often triggered by flashbacks and nightmares.

Symptoms like those common to attention deficit hyperactivity disorder (ADHD) can also be brought on by trauma. Trauma-related anxiety and similar symptoms, such as being unable to focus or sit still or constantly fidgeting, look very much like ADHD. Without knowledge of the trauma, or without very specialized training, it may be difficult to know or tell the difference—especially when children present these symptoms.

Addie

Addie jumps around so much that her professors complain that she is disrupting the class. She never focuses and she can't sit still, and two of her professors keep telling her that she should be evaluated for medication for her ADHD.

What they don't know is that Addie was beaten as a child and is living with a successful man, twelve years her senior, who is physically, mentally, emotionally, and sexually abusing her. Abuse is all Addie has ever known, and she is too terrified to tell anyone. It is likely that Addie is struggling with post-traumatic stress disorder, not ADHD.

An inability or lack of desire to make decisions, also called learned helplessness, can also be a cognitive symptom of trauma. As a result of being told over and over again that every decision he or she makes is wrong, bad, or stupid, a person will begin to stop (or want to stop) making decisions. This is especially true if the person is punished by his or her partner or other controlling family member for always making the wrong decisions. As a result, he or she relinquishes control to the partner or other controlling family member, allowing her or him to make all the decisions.

Part 4: Responses to Trauma

Fight or Flight Response

The fight or flight response (also referred to as the acute stress response) was discovered by the renowned Harvard physiologist Walter Cannon. The fight or flight response is the human body's primitive response to a perceived threat or attack to one's self. The body appears to go on automatic pilot, preparing to fight (defend itself), engage in flight (to run or flee), or freeze (to be unable to move) in response to a perceived attack, harm, or threat. When a person experiences a trauma, he or she automatically goes into the primal survival mode of the fight, flight, or freeze response (Brown and Fee, 2002, pp. 1594–1595).

Anger and Trauma

Anger and violence are not the same thing. Anger is an emotion. Violence is an unhealthy and often inappropriate behavior in response to the emotion of anger. Anger is what is called a secondary emotion. It does not exist by itself. When there is anger, it is *always* preceded by hurt, fear, or both. Anger is a way for a person to feel less vulnerable after feeling hurt and/or scared. An angry response can warn others away from your personal space.

Why is anger a common response to trauma? High levels of anger are related to a natural survival instinct. Along with fear, anger is a normal response to terror, to events that seem unfair, and to feeling out of control or victimized. Anger helps a person survive by mobilizing all his or her attention, thought, brain energy, and action toward survival. Anger is often a common response to betrayal or to losing basic trust in another person or persons, especially in situations of domestic and/or sexual violence. In addition, when the trauma experienced by a victim includes early childhood abuse, the trauma and shock of the abuse often interferes with his or her ability to regulate emotions. This may result in frequent episodes of emotions or outbursts that are out of control, including anger and rage.

Acute Stress Disorder and Domestic/Sexual Violence

Acute stress disorder (ASD) is a clinical diagnosis given to an individual who has experienced a traumatic event and develops anxiety-related symptoms, such as reexperiencing the traumatic event and/or avoiding stimuli related to the event. ASD is very similar to PTSD; the main differential criterion is the amount of time between the symptoms and the trauma. The clinical diagnosis of acute stress disorder is given when the symptoms occur within the first four weeks after a traumatic event and resolve during the first six months. A clinical diagnosis of post-traumatic stress disorder is given when the above symptoms last six months after the trauma or longer.

PTSD and Domestic and/or Sexual Violence

Post-traumatic stress disorder (PTSD) is often a normal response to an abnormal life-threatening or perceived to be life-threatening traumatic event. It is a mental health disorder that develops as a result of a horrific, life-threatening, or otherwise traumatic experience. PTSD sufferers reexperience the traumatic event or events by way of flashbacks, vivid nightmares, memories, and so on. People who suffer from PTSD tend to avoid places, people, or other things that remind them of the event and are overly sensitive to what others perceive as normal life experiences or sensory-related triggers, such as door slamming, odors or scents, a touch on the arm, etc. Although the symptoms of PTSD have long been problematic for those who have experienced a major trauma, PTSD has only been recognized as a formal diagnosis since 1980.

What is PTSD, and what is its connection to victims of intimate partner violence? Beginning in the late 1980s and early 1990s, researchers Astin, Lawrence, and Foy began to recognize and affirm a clinical link between intimate partner violence and PTSD (Astin, Lawrence, and Foy, 1993). Victims of intimate partner violence often experience a high level of violence and/or frequent exposure to violence, which causes trauma-related symptoms. In addition, the violence is perpetrated by someone whom the victim loves, trusts, and often has had children with. PTSD is not only a result of the physical, emotional, psychological, and/or sexual violence that a victim of domestic violence has already experienced in the relationship; it is also the result of the partner's controlling, manipulative, and isolating actions that cause continued fear for the victim's safety. This ongoing fear increases the likelihood that a victim of domestic violence will develop PTSD. Research reveals that the prevalence of PTSD among victims of domestic violence has been as high as 63.8 percent (Cascardi, O'Leary, and Schlee, 1999). Consequently, it is critical to remember that the related trauma experienced by victims of domestic violence often negatively alters their sense of trust, safety, and self-worth.

It cannot be stressed enough that the responses and symptoms listed in this chapter are normal responses to an abnormal event and should be thought of that way. They, and the person who is experiencing them, are not to be criticized or judged—only to be understood.

Assessing for Domestic Violence and Lethality

Amy and Alan

Amy and Alan are in an abusive and controlling relationship. In addition to his abusive and controlling ways, Alan watches a lot of pornography and won't have sex with Amy unless she watches it with him. She doesn't mind watching it now and then but says, "Not every time!" Amy thinks that Alan "has a problem or a porn addiction." Amy has threatened to leave the relationship if Alan doesn't get help. Alan tells her that after she had the kids and put on "all that weight," she is not sexy enough to get him aroused anymore. When they go to see a couple's counselor, Amy doesn't say much at first due to her fear of being punished when they get home. The counselor says the therapy will only work if she is honest, and so she is. As she had feared, she is later punished by Alan for, as he puts it, "making me look like a stupid sex addict in front of the counselor."

W hen it comes to the outcome of intimate partner relationships or the safety of their victims, there are no crystal balls or guarantees. There are, however, ways to assess the lethality of the situation and the relationship. Once lethality is determined, then the specifics of a safety plan can be created and implemented accordingly.

Intimate Partner Lethality Assessment

Section 1

1. How long have you and your partner been together? (The longer the abuse has been going on, the more beaten down and desensitized the victim may be.)
2. What was the relationship like in the beginning? (If it seemed too good to be true, it probably was.)
3. What is the relationship like now? How is it the same as and/or different from it was in the beginning? (If you would describe the early part of the relationship as "wonderful," "perfect," and/or "so romantic" in the beginning but would say that the relationship changed as soon as you went from dating to being in a relationship, that's a big red flag for an abusive and/or controlling relationship.)
4. Is your partner controlling? If so, how? (The more controlling your partner is, the more potential for him or her to escalate if you try to leave and take the control back.)
5. Is your partner very jealous? If so, what happens when he or she gets jealous? (Jealousy and related accusations, especially related to having sex, affairs, or fantasies, about other men and/or women, can be big red flags for controlling abusive partners and are often followed by a violent or aggressive outburst.)
6. Does your partner verbally accuse you and degrade you about things he or she thinks you did or want to do? Or does your partner punish you in some way for these things?

The harsher the accusations and related punishments, the higher the potential for lethality.)

7. Does your partner need to know where you are at all times? If so, what happens if you are out too long? (This is a byproduct of jealousy and a need for control. The more he or she complains and/or punishes you for getting home late from the grocery store, picking up the kids, or working too late, the higher the potential for lethality.)

8. Does your partner treat you the same as or differently from he or she does other people? If so, how? (If your partner is a Dr. Jekyll and Mr./Ms. Hyde type, this means that he or she can control his or her anger and chooses not to. He or she chooses control. Also, this type of abuser wants the world to believe he or she is a good, kind, and loving person and partner. The more his or her control is challenged, the more abusive this person is likely to become.)

9. Does your partner treat you differently around other people from when you are alone? If so how? (Someone who will treat you in an abusive and/or controlling manner in front of other people is a person who believes that she or he is above consequences, or she or he no longer cares if anyone knows how she or he is treating you. This makes her or him more dangerous.)

10. Have you ever wanted or needed to call for help but were afraid to do so? What happened? (If you were afraid to get help, it is likely because you are aware of the potential for danger. When you are ready and feel it is safe to do so, try again.)

11. What do you think your partner would say or do if he or she knew that you were talking with a counselor or therapist? (If you are doing so and fear you'll be punished for it, then create a safety plan with your therapist, just in case he or she finds out, and know that this is another red flag for increased lethality.)

Section 2: Types of Abuse

1. Emotional abuse. Has your partner ever (circle all that apply):

    - controlled your activities?
    - attacked your self-esteem?
    - intentionally frightened you?
    - destroyed your property?
    - verbally abused you?
    - called you names?
    - made you feel crazy?
    - screamed and yelled at you?
    - punched a wall in front of you?
    - done anything else upsetting that you can think of?

2. Psychological abuse. Has your partner ever threatened to (circle all that apply):

    - take away your children?
    - hurt your children?
    - hurt your family or friends?
    - hurt you?
    - hurt or kill himself or herself?
    - kill the children?
    - destroy property?
    - do anything else upsetting?

    Has he or she ever followed through on any threats? If so, how?

3. Isolation. Has your partner ever (circle all that apply):

- kept you from going to work?
- kept you from going to school?
- kept you from going to church or other religious services?
- kept you from going to meetings?
- kept you from going out with friends or family?
- listened to your phone calls?
- opened or checked your e-mail and/or your phone?
- followed you around?
- questioned your whereabouts?
- moved you away from your family against your wishes?

4. Physical abuse. Has your partner ever (circle all that apply):

- hit you?
- kicked you?
- thrown you around?
- slapped you?
- cut you?
- shot you?
- pushed you?
- choked you?
- pulled your hair?
- twisted your arm?
- burned you?
- smothered you?
- punched you?
- restrained you?
- thrown things at you?

Has your partner ever hurt you physically in any other way? If so how?

5. Sexual abuse/coercion. Has your partner ever (circle all that apply):

- forced you to have sex?
- tied you up against your will?
- used objects during sex against your will?
- attacked your sexual body parts?
- treated you like a sex object?
- forced uncomfortable acts upon you?
- accused you of having affairs?
- called you a whore or a slut?
- withheld sexual affection from you?
- had affairs?

The more examples you circled, the higher the likelihood that you are in an abusive relationship and the higher the potential for violence and/or lethality as the relationship continues or if you choose to leave. Regardless, if you found yourself saying yes to any more than one or two of these questions, please, whether you choose to stay in or leave the relationship, talk to someone about creating a safety plan.

Section 3: History of Violence and/or Abuse

Please answer the following:

1. Has your partner threatened to kill you, himself or herself, or the children?
   If so, how would he or she plan to do it? Under what circumstances?
   Do you believe your partner is capable of killing you?

Do you believe your partner is capable of killing another person?
Have you ever been afraid your partner would kill you? If so, how?
Does your partner have weapons or access to weapons?

These are all big red flags for a high level of lethality.

2. Does your partner have fits of rage? If so, what happens? Fits of rage and issues with control, or with losing it, can be a very lethal combination.

3. Does your partner appear obsessed with you? If yes, describe.
    The more obsessed he or she is with you, the greater the chance of him or her believing that you belong to him or her and the less likely he or she is to let you leave without punishment or consequences.

4. Do you believe your partner uses drugs or alcohol? If yes, how often?
    Often people who have trouble controlling their use of drugs and/or alcohol also have trouble with controlling their partners. Also, when a person is under the influence, the rational thinking filter is removed and the escalation of physical violence is often more likely and more dangerous.

5. Do you believe you can leave the house safely when the abuse begins to escalate?
    Not everyone living with an abusive partner is ready (or feels able) to leave right away. If this is you, please come up with a plan to be able to leave when the violence begins to escalate and then return when it's safer for you to do so. If it is not safe to leave, then come up with the

safest plan that you can within the house (and include your children in your plan if you have any living in the home with you).

6. Do you believe you can take your children with you safely when the abuse begins to escalate? If no, why not?
This is a tough one. If your partner is abusive to you and not to the children, sometimes it's safer to leave the children, get out, and then get them when it's safer to do. This does not mean that you are abandoning your children. Your partner is still their parent, and unless the Department of Youth Services is involved (due to the confirmed witnessing of domestic violence or child abuse), you will likely get joint custody if you choose to leave the relationship anyway. You may wish to call law enforcement and have them escort you back to the house to get the children.

7. How long have you been with your partner?
The longer you have been together, and the longer the behavior has been going on, the more empowered your partner feels and the less likely he or she believes you will leave, at least for good.

8. How long has your relationship been abusive?
The longer the relationship has been abusive, the more likely it is that the violence will escalate and the less likely the controlling partner will be willing to give up control over you. Your partner will often feel that you belong to him or her and will not be willing to lose control or what (or who) he or she believes belongs to him or her.

9. When was your partner's first abusive behavior toward you (see list above if needed)?
See next question.

10. When was the most recent incident? What happened? How much has your partner escalated from the first to the most recent (or even another recent) incident?
The higher the escalation, the higher the lethality risk.

11. How frequently is your partner abusive in the following ways? Fill in the blanks.
Physically: _____
Emotionally: _____
Psychologically (threats): _____
Sexually: _____
In terms of destroying property:_____
In terms of hurting pets?_____

Again, the higher the number, the higher the lethality. Even if there has been no physical violence, but there has been extreme mental or emotional abuse, it is likely that physical violence could occur should you try to leave and take control back. Safety planning is still necessary.

12. Does it seem that the threats are occurring more frequently?
If so, this is a big red flag for escalation of lethality and the need for safety planning.

13. Does it seem that the abuse is getting worse?
Pain and abuse are not contests, but *worse* means more dangerous and more need for coming up with a safety plan. You need a safety plan for staying in the relationship and another one for leaving it.

14. Has your partner ever been violent with law enforcement? Violent with others? If yes, with whom?

If your partner has been violent with law enforcement, that often means he or she no longer cares about consequences or truly struggles with controlling, or wanting to control, his or her behavior. If your partner is only violent with you (and perhaps his or her other ex-partners), that means the problem is not with anger but with control. It likely will escalate if and when you try to leave and take back control.

15. Have you ever called law enforcement for assistance because of abuse? If yes, what happened?
    If law enforcement was called, your partner was arrested, and then he or she got out the next day and punished you for calling, then the likelihood of your calling them again is minimal. Also, if your partner got off and nothing happened—or worse, your partner lied to the police and you got arrested (or you both got arrested)—then you are unlikely to call again.

16. Has your partner ever been arrested for domestic violence (against you or a partner other than you)? If yes, has there ever been an injunction for protection (IFP), restraining order (RO), or no contact order (NCO) put in place? If yes, by whom?
    If your partner has been arrested for domestic violence or is violent even when knowing that there is an IFP, NCO, or RO, then lethality is increased because he or she cares more about hurting, injuring, or otherwise punishing you than about going to jail.

17. Have you ever obtained an injunction for protection? If yes, what happened?
    The best predictor of future behavior is past behavior—and/or an escalated version of past behavior.

18. Do you feel you need an IFP now?
Trust your gut. If you feel it will escalate the violence, wait. Remember, your partner will get a copy of everything you write about him or her, and that too often escalates abusive and violent behaviors.

19. Is or was there abuse in your partner's family of origin? If yes, describe. Domestic violence is a learned behavior. It is not 100 percent guaranteed, but like the flu virus, the more that a person is exposed to it, the higher the risk of catching it—or repeating the behavior.

20. Is there a warrant out on your partner? If yes, where, and for what? Is your partner on probation? If yes, for what? This relates to your partner's moral character, his or her likelihood or fear of going to jail, and/or his or her possible feelings of a lack of control over his or her life.

21. Please state your partner education level. PhDs are often victims and abusers, but the higher the education level, the greater the fear of going to jail.

22. Is your partner employed? If yes, where? Doing what? Is he or she afraid of the stigma of jail, losing his or her job, or losing an employment-related certification or license if he or she is convicted of a violence-related offense? If so, the lethality in this case may be lower.

It is important to note that if the person causing the bruises no longer cares where the bruises are or if anyone can see them, the lethality increases significantly.

The next chapter focuses on safety planning. If you found yourself identifying with or saying yes to a number of the above questions, then you are likely at risk. The more controlling your partner is, the higher the lethality risk when you try to leave. Chapter 8 will help you learn how to create and implement a safety plan. If you are in a controlling or abusive relationship, whether you choose to stay or leave, please create a safety plan before you need one. Help is available if you want or need it. (See the resource index located in the back of this book.)

8 Safety Planning with Victims of Intimate Partner Violence

When a person is in a controlling relationship and wants (or tries) to leave, the abusive and/or controlling partner's violent behavior often will escalate. When the victim leaves, the abusive partner loses control over the victim, which makes him or her angry and often violent. The abusive partner will likely try to punish the victim for leaving (or trying to).

Working with victims of domestic violence for twenty-five years in private practice and in domestic violence shelters has taught me that safety planning is critical, whether you are choosing to stay or thinking of leaving a controlling and/or abusive relationship. And even if there has never been physical violence, that doesn't mean there can't or won't be.

Here Are Some Tips

When things start to escalate, stay out of kitchens (where there are knives) and bathrooms (where you can be trapped and a fall can be fatal).

Assemble a bag with important items you would need if you had to make a quick escape (passport and other ID, extra keys, cash, medication, birth certificates, and other important papers).

It is best to keep this with a friend or in another safe place outside of your home.

During a conflict, get to a room with a door that will allow you to escape. Alternatively, go to a room with a door you can lock from the inside and call 911.

Teach your children not to get in the middle of a fight, even if they want to help.

Devise a code word to use with your children, family, and friends when you need the police. Document signs of physical abuse.

Take photographs of injuries or bruises. Take care in contacting an agency for help. When calling a hotline, shelter, or agency from home, dial a 1-800 number immediately afterward to protect yourself in the event that your abuser dials a callback code like *69.

When using the Internet, do not use your home computer. Go to a library, an Internet café, or the like. If you do use your home computer, remember to erase your history and cache.

Protecting Yourself Once You Have Left

Leaving a controlling and abusive relationship does not ensure that the abuse will end. In fact, the opposite is often true, and the abuse escalates when the victim leaves. Here are a few tips to help you (or your friend or family member) stay safe:

Change your number or block his or hers (unless you have children or believe that this will escalate the violence, which it sometimes does). You know your partner better than anyone, so trust your gut on this one and on everything else.

Have someone who is knowledgeable about technology help you make sure that you are not being hacked, tracked, or cyberstalked. Check your phones, computers, tablets, and other technology to be sure there is no spyware. Many abusive partners create and/or install an electronic leash on their partners.

If your partner has moved out or if you do not live together, alert your neighbors, friends, and/or coworkers to call the police if they see him or her nearby. Create a signal that will tell them they should call.

Change the locks.

Provide a photo of your ex-partner to coworkers and security at your place of employment. If there are safety issues related to your children, bring both a photograph and copy of the restraining order (RSO), injunction for protection (IFP), or no-contact order (NCO), if you have them, to your children's teachers and school administrators. Advise them not to allow him or her on the premises.

Make sure your child's school and your employer know not to give your address or phone number to anyone.

Change your habits. Shop at different stores. Shop at different times. Vary your schedule as much as possible.

At work, have a security guard accompany you to your car.

If you have left without the help of authorities, a domestic violence hotline, or other domestic violence agency, contact them now for help and advice on staying safe.

Mandated Reporting

Whether you are a victim of domestic violence or a professional working with victims and/or their children, it is critical that you understand what mandated reporting is and what it is not.

As of August 2015, forty-eight of the fifty United States, in addition to the District of Columbia, American Samoa, Guam, the Northern Mariana Islands, Puerto Rico, and the American Virgin Islands, designate professionals whose members are mandated by law to report child maltreatment (abuse, neglect, and/or failure to protect).[7] In the state of Florida, where I live, chapter 39 of the Florida Statutes mandates that "any person who knows, or has reasonable cause to suspect, that a child is abused, abandoned, or neglected by a parent, legal custodian, caregiver, or other person responsible for the child's welfare, shall report immediately such knowledge or suspicion to the central abuse hotline of the Department of Children and Families (DCF)."[8] Mandated reporters, including counselors, teachers, and medical professionals, are required to tell victims of domestic violence that they risk having their children removed for "failure to protect" if they don't leave a physically abusive partner when the children are subjected to or witnesses to violence in the home or if they knowingly don't report or leave a relationship where there a child is being physically or sexually abused,

If you are a professional working with a victim who has reported domestic violence where children are at risk (or has reported child abuse), remind the victim of her or his responsibility to protect her or his children and the limits to confidentiality as outlined in the initial intake discussion or form the victim agreed to and signed.

Even if the victim is an adult, he or she is likely to have negative (and sometimes even dangerous) consequences for disclosing the abuse. As soon as the investigators contact the perpetrator, or shortly after they leave, the victim will likely be punished for telling the authorities on the partner and, as some abusers might put it, "lying and trying to get my ass in trouble" and/or "putting my business out it the street."

Remember that the victim is likely to be frightened and angry and may now feel violated again by yet another person the victim trusted. Respecting the victim enough to tell her or him that you are going to make the call to the child abuse hotline and what is likely to happen next will help them feel believed and supported. Safety planning with the victim is critical, and telling the victim that you are calling in a report can also help her or him not feel betrayed and/or blindsided by an unexpected visit from the authorities. If the person disclosing is a child, he or she doesn't have a voice or a choice as to where to go or who to stay with. Assessing safety and those who can assist in implementing a safety plan is critical because victim lethality is likely to escalate once the call has been made.

A professional must never tell a victim or a child that "everything will be fine," as he or she does not know that it will be, and often it is not. Don't make statements and promises that are untrue or that cannot be kept.

Domestic Violence and the Courts

T he legal system handles domestic violence cases in various courts. Criminal court handles domestic violence arrests, family court handles divorce and custody cases, civil court handles injunctions for protection or restraining orders, and dependency court handles child abuse, neglect, and failure-to-protect cases. In many states, each court system has its own judge and area of jurisdiction, and although a domestic case may be presented in more than one court, each case is legally handled independently of the others, with little crossover ruling from one court to the next.

Criminal Courts

Barry and Victoria

Barry was arrested for throwing a beer bottle at Victoria. He was let out of jail the next morning. As a result of Barry's violent behavior and related arrest, the judge ordered no contact between Barry and Victoria. Victoria believed that Barry was only violent because, according to her, he'd "had too many beers." Barry agreed to go to AA and told Victoria that he was sorry and promised it would never happen again.

Victoria believed Barry and went to court to try to drop the restraining order against him. She believed that Barry needed counseling, not jail. Victoria told the judge that Barry had "admitted he was sorry and said it would never happen again. He even agreed to go to counseling." When Victoria went to the safety class that was mandatory for dropping the injunction, she learned that she couldn't drop it, because he had been arrested and had a no-contact order (NCO), not a restraining order or injunction for protecting (IFP). Because of the arrest and the type of order, the rules were different (and so were the specifics as to how to modify or drop it).

After an arrest is made, judges often issue a no-contact order. The terms *no-contact order, injunction,* and *restraining order* are often used interchangeably. Although they are similar, they are not the same. A judge issues a no-contact order following an arrest for domestic violence. An injunction for protection, which is commonly referred to as a restraining order, is a civil petition by the victim to the court, requesting that a perpetrator of domestic violence have no (or limited) contact with the victim due to a past history of threats and/or violence. Victims often don't know what type of contact order they have and often confuse the two. They often report having an injunction for protection or restraining order when in fact they have a no-contact order. If a victim wishes to drop an IFP or NCO, it is imperative that she or he know which one she or he has. The steps that must be followed to drop or modify vary by order, as well as by state.

It is important to understand that injunctions are not always able to keep a victim safe. In fact, often perpetrators' behaviors escalate when they are served, because the victim is taking back control (or taking away control from the perpetrator), which often increases lethality. The lethality often increases for the victim following the perpetrator being served with an IFP or restraining order—especially when the controlling partner does not care about being incarcerated and cares more about control and/or revenge than consequences.

Family Court

Married victims who choose to leave and/or divorce their partners/spouses must do so through family court. Family court is where divorce, custody, and paternity cases are handled. Many courts and related professionals believe that domestic violence cases are the same as high-conflict cases, but this is often not the case.

Drew, Diane, and Daisy

Drew wanted to win custody of his eight-year-old daughter, Daisy. It's not that he wanted to spend time with her; he just wanted to win. In fact, he was so sure he was going to win that he had a full-time nanny on standby to take care of Daisy as soon as the court gave him full custody. His soon-to-be ex-wife, Diane, was very close with Daisy. He knew that Daisy was the most important person in Diane's life and wanted to punish Diane the most painful way possible for leaving him. In addition, Drew thought of Daisy as *his* daughter. He believed that she belonged to him. He thought of her more as a possession than a person, and he would make sure she would stay with him, even if her mother would not.

Divorcing couples where there is a history of domestic violence (a significant power differential in the relationship) are *not* in the same category as high-conflict cases. Legal and/or related clinical professionals should never categorize them as "non-cooperating" nor "high-conflict" divorcing couples. Categorizing them as high-conflict cases may mask or minimize serious safety issues and concerns for victims of domestic violence.

The court often uses the term *high-conflict case* when describing divorcing non-cooperative couples. Domestic violence is a control-related issue, not a conflict-related one. In situations and relationships in which there is or has been domestic violence, the conflict at hand is often merely a symptom of a much larger issue of control, a need for the controlling and/or abusive partner to win. Conflict resolution is only a workable option when both parties want to solve the problem. With domestic violence, there is only winning and losing, and the abusive partner wants to win and have his or needs and/or wants met without any thought or regard for anyone else.

This is why mediation may not be safe or effective for victims of domestic violence. Resolution is about the abusive partner getting what he or she wants, not about coming to a fair and mutually agreeable decision. Generally, the victim gives in or is punished for not giving in, not allowing the abusive partner to win, and taking back some control. Although domestic violence is a predominant characteristic of high-conflict divorcing couples, a significant number of high-conflict cases do not include domestic violence. These high-conflict cases may involve parents whose rigid personality styles or even mental health difficulties have them trapped in prolonged litigation. In addition, divorcing couples in high-conflict cases may have fundamental differences with respect to religious beliefs, culture, parenting philosophies/ styles, and/or medical care. These cases differ from more typical separation conflicts because one or both parents are willing to expend emotional and financial resources in litigation, often on a mission of revenge or validation. While most divorcing couples find reasonable stability and are able to begin moving forward in their new co-parenting roles after a two-to-three-year period, these high-conflict couples remain enemies and maintain the legal conflict and emotional entanglement for many years to come.

Unfortunately, domestic violence divorces are often characterized as being high-conflict cases or isolated, uncharacteristic incidents caused by the distress of a separation rather than being recognized as risk markers for severe or even lethal violence in the context of a pattern of historical abuse.

In addition, when the victim of domestic violence is the custodial parent or the co-parent, she or he is frequently faced with attaining and maintaining a safe place for herself or himself and the children. Therefore, court-ordered joint custody and/or visitations with the abusive parent find the victims emotionally and mentally distraught and concerned about the safety of their children. To the victim, it often feels like a choice between violating the court order or putting the children at risk.

Lisa and Lefty

Lisa and Lefty were together fifteen years and had two children, twelve-year-old Gretta and nine-year-old Gary. Lisa finally had had enough and told Lefty she was leaving him. Lefty threatened that if she left he would take the kids away from her and ruin her life any way he could. She felt that he'd already ruined her life, and she couldn't take it anymore.

Lisa had been isolated from her sister Lina for five years because Lefty was angry that after, as he put it, "the one mistake I made years ago," describing an incident of domestic violence "when Lisa made him so mad," he'd grabbed her and pushed her into the wall. At that time, Lisa's sister couldn't be there fast enough to help her pack her belongings and leave with the kids. He threatened Lisa not to be in contact with her sister anymore.

Despite Lefty's threats, Lisa contacted her sister for help and filed for divorce the next day. Five years and many counseling sessions later, Lisa is in a healthy relationship with Henry, who loves her and her children, and they are expecting a child of their own.

Human beings don't get to choose who we love; we only get to choose how we behave.

Loving someone does not mean having to accept unacceptable behavior.

If you love someone who is trying to manipulate, control, or disempower you, that is unacceptable behavior. Staying is a choice, but so is leaving. There is life, and healing, after domestic violence. Talking with a professional counselor who is trained in intimate partner violence and/or abuse (remember that emotional and mental abuse are still abuse) can help you heal and move forward. It is possible to have a healthy, loving relationship with yourself and, as a result, create a stronger likelihood for a next relationship that is healthy and empowering instead unhealthy, disempowering, and abusive.

If you have been isolated to the point where you no longer feel you have a support system, or one that you can trust, every county and state has shelters—many with outpatient counseling, advocacy, and case management services available—as well as human services agencies, religious organizations, law enforcement agencies, and other resources available to help. (See below for a list of some available options.)

One Last Story

U p until this point, every story you have read is a fictionalized composite of real stories. There is one more story I need to tell—my own. I was in a very unhealthy and abusive relationship. For six years, I dated and then married Felix (not his real name). We met in college just prior to my graduation. For much of our relationship, I loved Felix more than I loved myself. One day I realized that my relationship and life with Felix were not going to get better; they would only get worse, as would my pain. I noticed that his abusive words and behaviors had slowly escalated over time. I believed then, as I do now, that love is unconditional and that we don't get to choose whom we love. We just love whom we love, but we do get to choose how we behave and what type of behavior we are willing to accept. I knew I couldn't stop loving Felix, so I would just have to love him from someplace else.

When I told Felix I was leaving, he took an overdose of pills and told me he couldn't live without me. He knew that my father had died from a suicidal pill overdose when I was fourteen.

Felix didn't really want to die; he only wanted to manipulate me and trigger my past traumatic loss as a way of keeping me with him. He almost went too far. Thankfully, I left work, found him, and called 911. The first responders rushed him to the hospital, where they pumped him full of charcoal. I stayed by his side for three days until I knew he was going to live, and then I left.

When I was twenty-seven, I left Felix, along with almost everyone I knew and everything I owned. I left with two suitcases and a check for $175 in my wallet, moved from Massachusetts to Florida, and started my life over. At the time, my mother and stepfather were living in Florida. They turned their garage into a studio apartment, where I lived for three months until I had enough money to move. I got a job, an apartment, and began the best part of my life.

I had to work through all the pain, trauma, and loss I'd experienced earlier in my life, which was difficult and took more time than I wanted to it to, but I did it! At the time of writing this book, I have been very happily married for nineteen years (we've been together for twenty-one) to a man with whom I share a mutual love, trust, and respect—but before I found him, I had to find myself. I had to find my self-worth. It was always there, but I just couldn't see it. I found it, embraced it, and learned to believe that I was worthy not only of love but of respect as well.

Even if no one is physically hitting or punching you, if you are being hurt and/or are being made to feel afraid, you are in an abusive relationship. If you are unhappy or afraid, call a professional. Even if you don't want to leave or are just not ready to, call a professional. Abusive relationships don't make you crazy, but they certainly can make you *feel* crazy. This book is not meant to take the place of therapy. It's meant to open your eyes to what an abusive relationship is and looks like. If you saw yourself or your relationship anywhere in these pages, please consider talking with a professional who doesn't have a horse in the race, so to speak. A counselor can help you validate your feelings, help you further understand the dynamics of domestic violence, help assess (not judge) the lethality of your situation, and help you create a safety plan accordingly.

 **No More Myths: Truths Revealed**

B elow are answers to the quiz you took at the start of this book.

1. Myth: The victim always does something to provoke the abusive partner's violence. Truth: No one deserves to be beaten, battered, threatened, or in any way victimized by violence. Batterers will rarely admit that they are the cause of the problem or take any responsibility for it. In fact, putting the blame for the violence on the victim is one of the ways a controlling partner manipulates (and controls) the victim as well as other people. Batterers will tell their victims, "You made me so mad that I had to hit you" or "You made me jealous," or they will try to shift the burden by saying, "Everyone acts like that." Most victims try to placate and please their abusive partners in order to deescalate the violence. The batterer chooses to abuse and bears full responsibility for the violence.

2. Myth: Children who are not primary victims of domestic violence are not really affected by domestic violence. Truth: Children, especially those growing up in troubled homes, are smarter and more intuitive than many parents and/or professionals give them credit for. They may not

say anything, but that does not mean that they do not know about, understand, and suffer from the violence in the home—even at a very young age. When home, the one place a person is supposed to be and feel safe and protected, is a danger zone, then the rest of the world, and those in it, must be even scarier. The ability to trust and often to connect with others becomes more and more difficult for these children. They also learn that love hurts. Domestic violence is a learned behavior, and many of the children who grow up in violent homes grow up to be victims and abusers themselves. Indirectly, children are also affected by the domestic violence, in that the victimized parent is always trying to please the controlling and abusive partner, often to keep everyone safe, and has little time and/or energy left for the children or their needs.

3. Myth: Most batterers simply lose control during violent incidents and do not know what they're doing. Truth: If batterers were truly out of control, as many claim to be during violent incidents, there would be many more domestic violence homicides. In fact, many batterers do control their violence, abusing their victims in less visible places on their bodies, such as under the hairline or on the stomach (somewhere that clothes will always cover). Furthermore, researchers have found that domestic violence often occurs in cycles and that every episode is preceded by a predictable, repeated pattern of behavior and decisions made by the batterer.

4. Myth: When a couple is having a domestic violence problem, this just means the couple has a bad relationship. Often it's poor communication that is the problem. Truth: Bad relationships do not result in or cause domestic violence (emotional, mental, sexual, and/or physical abuse). The idea that bad relationships cause abuse is one of the most

common and dangerous misconceptions about domestic violence. First, it encourages all parties involved— including and especially the victim—to minimize the seriousness of the problem and focus their energies on improving the relationship, in the false hope that this will stop the abuse. It also allows the abuser to blame the bad relationship and the violence itself on the victim rather than acknowledging his or her own responsibility. More importantly, improving the relationship is not likely, by itself, to end the violence. Domestic violence is learned behavior. Many couples have had bad relationships that never resulted in abuse. Many batterers are violent in every one of their relationships, whether they consider each relationship to be bad or good. The abuser is the sole source and cause of the violence, and neither his or her partner nor their relationship should be held responsible.

5. Myth: Domestic violence is often triggered by stress, such as the loss of a job or some financial or marital problem. Truth: Daily life is full of frustrations associated with money and work, our families, and other personal relationships. Everyone experiences stress, and everyone responds to it differently. Violence is a specific learned and chosen response to stress, whether real or imagined. Certainly high incidents of domestic violence can be related to social problems, such as unemployment. However, other reactions to such situations are equally possible. The loss of control over social or environmental issues will increase an abusive partner's need for control in intimate partner relationships. Many people do not need to take out their stress and frustration on others with verbal (emotional/psychological) or physical abuse.

6. Myth: Most real domestic violence only occurs in poor, minority, and/or trailer park communities. Truth: Domestic violence occurs at all levels of society, regardless

of the abuser's (or victim's) social, economic, racial, or cultural backgrounds; however, economic and social factors may have a significant impact on how people respond to violent incidents and what kinds of help they seek or do not seek. People with money can often afford private help—doctors, lawyers, and counselors—while people with fewer financial resources, such as those belonging to a lower economic class, tend to call the police or other public agencies. These agencies are often the only available source of statistics on domestic violence, so lower class and minority communities tend to be overrepresented in those figures, creating a distorted image of the problem.

7. Myth: The use of intoxicating substances, such as drugs and/or alcohol, causes domestic violence. Truth: Just because physical violence may (and often does) only occur after the perpetrator has used drugs or alcohol does not mean that the violence is caused by the drugs or alcohol. Many people drink and/or use drugs without battering their partners. If drugs and/or alcohol caused domestic violence, then every person who drank or used drugs would batter their partner, which simply is not the case. If this were true, there would be no such thing as a happy drunk, which is a description often used to describe a person's disposition and behavior after consuming enough alcohol to meet the criteria for his or her being under the influence. Alcohol is often referred to as "liquid courage." It doesn't make people do things that they don't want to do, but it removes the filter and in some cases can escalate behaviors that are already there. Stopping the abuser's drinking will not stop the violence. Both battering and substance abuse need to be addressed separately as overlapping yet independent problems.

8. Myth: Just because violence occurs once in an intimate partner relationship does not mean it will happen again. Truth: Battering is a pattern of manipulation and control that one intimate partner exerts over another. Battering is not just one physical attack. It includes the repeated use of a number of tactics, including intimidation, threats, economic deprivation, isolation, and psychological and sexual abuse. Physical violence is just one of these tactics. The various forms of abuse that batterers utilize help maintain power and control over their spouses and partners.

9. Myth: Victims of domestic violence must like and/or provoke the abuse. If not, they would refuse to take it and just leave. Truth: Victim provocation of violence is no more common in domestic violence than in any other crime. Battered women or men often make repeated attempts to leave violent relationships but are prevented from doing so by increased violence and control tactics on the part of the abuser. Other factors that inhibit a victim's ability to leave include economic dependence, few viable options for housing and support, unhelpful responses from the criminal justice system or other agencies, social isolation, cultural or religious constraints, a commitment to the abuser and the relationship, and fear of further violence. It has been estimated that the danger to a victim increases by 70 percent when she or he attempts to leave, as the abuser escalates the use of violence when the abuser begins to lose control.[5]

10. Myth: Men are victims of domestic violence as often as women, even if they don't report it. Truth: The bottom line is that domestic violence is a crime—regardless of the gender of the abuser or the victim and regardless of whether it is a heterosexual or same-sex relationship. Data from the FBI and the Bureau of Justice Statistics show that

85 percent of primary victims of intimate partner violence (IPV) are women. Acknowledging this indisputable fact does not negate our concern for the men who comprise the remaining 15 percent of IPV victims.[6]

11. Myth: Domestic violence is a less serious problem—less lethal—than "real" violence, such as street crimes. Truth: It is a terrible and unrecognized fact that for many people, home is the least safe place. Domestic violence accounts for a significant proportion of all serious crimes, including aggravated assault, rape, and homicide. Furthermore, when compared with stranger-on-stranger crime, the rate of occurrence and levels of severity are still under reported for domestic violence.

12. Myth: Where there is domestic violence, both parties are participants and are therefore responsible for the violence. For this reason, both parties are responsible for stopping the violence. Truth: Only the batterer has the ability to stop the violence. Battering is a behavioral choice for which the batterer must be held accountable. Many battered partners make numerous attempts to change their behavior in the hope that this will stop the abuse. They blame themselves and not their partner for the violence. This does not work. The victim does not cause the battering; therefore, he or she cannot stop it from happening.

APPENDIX A

The Diagnostic and Statistical Manual of Mental Disorders (5th ed.; DSM-5; American Psychiatric Association, 2013) is the most widely accepted nomenclature used by clinicians and researchers for the classification of mental disorders. Here is the DSM-V criteria for acute stress disorder:

DSM-V Criteria for Acute Stress Disorder (ASD)

The American Psychiatric Association's *Diagnostic and Statistical Manual of Mental Disorders, Fifth Edition (DSM-5)*, lists 5 specific diagnostic criteria for ASD.

The first criterion is exposure to actual or threatened death, serious injury, or sexual violation in one (or more) of the following ways:

- Directly experiencing the traumatic events(s)
- Witnessing, in person, the event(s) happening to others
- Learning that the event(s) occurred to a close family member or close friend (in cases of actual or threatened death of a family member or friend, the event[s] must have been violent or accidental)
- Experiencing repeated or extreme exposure to aversive details of the traumatic event(s) (such as first responders

collecting human remains or police officers repeatedly being exposed to details of child abuse)

The second criterion is the presence of at least nine of fourteen symptoms from any of five categories—intrusion, negative mood, dissociation, avoidance, and arousal—beginning or worsening after the traumatic event(s) occurred.

Intrusion symptoms include the following:

- Recurrent, involuntary, and intrusive distressing memories of the traumatic event(s); children may engage in repetitive play during which themes or aspects of the traumatic event(s) are expressed
- Recurrent distressing dreams in which the content or affect of the dream is related to the event(s); children may experience frightening dreams without recognizable content
- Dissociative reactions (such as flashbacks) in which the individual feels or acts as if the traumatic event(s) were recurring
- Intense or prolonged psychological distress or marked physiologic reactions in response to internal or external cues that symbolize or resemble an aspect of the traumatic event(s)

Negative mood consists of the following:

- Persistent inability to experience positive emotions (such as an inability to experience happiness, satisfaction, or loving feelings)

Dissociative symptoms include the following:

- Altered sense of the reality of one's surroundings or oneself (such as seeing oneself from another's perspective, being in a daze, or feeling that time is slowing)
- Inability to remember an important aspect of the traumatic event(s), typically resulting from dissociative amnesia and not from other factors (such as head injury, alcohol, or drugs)

Avoidance symptoms include the following:

- Efforts to avoid distressing memories, thoughts, or feelings about or closely associated with the traumatic event(s)
- Efforts to avoid external reminders (such as people, places, conversations, activities, objects, or situations) that arouse distressing memories, thoughts, or feelings about or closely associated with the traumatic event(s)

Arousal symptoms include the following:

- Sleep disturbance (such as difficulty falling or staying asleep or restlessness during sleep)
- Irritable behavior and angry outbursts (with little or no provocation), typically expressed as verbal or physical aggression toward people or objects
- Hypervigilance
- Problems with concentration
- Exaggerated startle response

The third *DSM-5* diagnostic criterion for ASD is that the duration of the disturbance is three days to one month after trauma exposure. Although symptoms may begin immediately after a traumatic event, they must last at least three days for a diagnosis of ASD to be made.

The fourth criterion is that the disturbance causes clinically significant distress or impairment in social, occupational, or other important areas of functioning.

The fifth and final criterion is that the disturbance cannot be attributed to the physiologic effects of a substance (such as a medication or alcohol) or another medical condition (such as mild traumatic brain injury) and cannot be better explained by a diagnosis of brief psychotic disorder.

ASD may progress to PTSD after one month, but it may also be a transient condition that resolves within one month of exposure to the traumatic event(s) and does not lead to PTSD. In about 50 percent of people who eventually develop PTSD, the initial presenting condition was ASD. Symptoms of ASD may worsen over the initial month, often as a consequence of ongoing stressors or additional traumatic events.

APPENDIX B

The Diagnostic and Statistical Manual of Mental Disorders (5th ed.; DSM-5; American Psychiatric Association, 2013) is the most widely accepted nomenclature used by clinicians and researchers for the classification of mental disorders. Here is the DSM-V criteria for post-traumatic stress disorder:

DSM-V Criteria for Post-Traumatic Stress Disorder (PTSD)

A. Exposure to actual or threatened death, serious injury, or sexual violence in one (or more) of the following ways:

1. Directly experiencing the traumatic event(s)
2. Witnessing, in person, the event(s) as the event(s) occurred to others
3. Learning that the traumatic event(s) occurred to a close family member or close friend. In cases of the actual or threatened death of a family member or friend, the event(s) must have been violent or accidental
4. Experiencing repeated or extreme exposure to aversive details of the traumatic event(s) (such as first responders collecting human remains or police officers repeatedly exposed to details of child abuse)

Note

Criterion A4 does not apply to exposure through electronic media, television, movies, or pictures, unless this exposure is work related.

B. Presence of one (or more) of the following intrusion symptoms associated with the traumatic event(s), beginning after the traumatic event(s) occurred:

1. Recurrent, involuntary, and intrusive distressing memories of the traumatic event(s)
2. Recurrent distressing dreams in which the content and/ or affect of the dream are related to the traumatic event(s)
3. Dissociative reactions (such as flashbacks) in which the individual feels or acts as if the traumatic event(s) were recurring; such reactions may occur on a continuum, with the most extreme expression being a complete loss of awareness of present surroundings
4. Intense or prolonged psychological distress at exposure to internal or external cues that symbolize or resemble an aspect of the traumatic event(s)
5. Marked psychological reactions to internal or external cues that symbolize or resemble an aspect of the traumatic event(s)

C. Persistent avoidance of stimuli associated with the traumatic event(s), beginning after the traumatic event(s) occurred, as evidenced by one or both of the following:

1. Avoidance of or efforts to avoid distressing memories, thoughts, or feelings about or closely associated with the traumatic event(s)

2. Avoidance of or efforts to avoid external reminders (such as people, places, conversations, activities, objects, and situations) that arouse distressing memories, thoughts, or feelings about or closely associated with the traumatic event(s)

D. Negative alterations in cognitions and mood associated with the traumatic event(s), beginning or worsening after the traumatic event(s) occurred, as evidenced by two (or more) of the following:

1. Inability to remember an important aspect of the traumatic event(s) (typically due to dissociative amnesia and not to other factors, such as head injury, alcohol, or drugs)
2. Persistent and exaggerated negative beliefs or expectations about oneself, others, or the world (such as "I am bad," "No one can be trusted," "The world is completely dangerous," or "My whole nervous system is permanently ruined")
3. Persistent, distorted cognitions about the cause or consequences of the traumatic event(s) that lead the individual to blame himself or herself or to blame others
4. Persistent negative emotional state (such as fear, horror, anger, guilt, or shame)
5. Markedly diminished interest or participation in significant activities
6. Feelings of detachment or estrangement from others
7. Persistent inability to experience positive emotions (such as an inability to experience happiness, satisfaction, or loving feelings)

E. Marked alterations in arousal and reactivity associated with the traumatic event(s), beginning or worsening after the traumatic event(s) occurred, as evidenced by two (or more) of the following:

1. Irritable behavior and angry outbursts (with little or no provocation), typically expressed as verbal or physical aggression toward people or objects
2. Reckless or self-destructive behavior
3. Hypervigilance
4. Exaggerated startle response
5. Problems with concentration
6. Sleep disturbance (such as difficulty falling or staying asleep or restless sleep)

F. Duration of the disturbance (criteria B, C, D, and E) is more than one month.

G. The disturbance causes clinically significant distress or impairment in social, occupational, or other important areas of functioning.

H. The disturbance is not attributable to the physiological effects of a substance (such as medication or alcohol) or another medical condition.

HELPFUL LINKS AND CONTACTS

RESOURCE INDEX

Bureau of Justice Statistics (BJS)
810 Seventh Street, NW
Washington, DC 20531
United States
Phone: 202-307-0765
Fax: 202-307-5849
http://www.ojp.usdoj.gov/bjs

Child Welfare Information Gateway
Children's Bureau/ACYF
1250 Maryland Avenue, SW, 8th Floor
Washington, DC 20024
United States
Phone: 800.394.3366
E-mail: info@childwelfare.gov
http://www.childwelfare.gov

National Center for Injury Prevention and Control
Centers for Disease Control and Prevention
1600 Clifton Road
Atlanta, GA 30329-4027

United States
Phone: 770-488-1506
Fax: 770-488-1667
cdc.gov/injury/index.html
e-mail: CDC-INFO

National Criminal Justice Reference Service (NCJRS)
PO Box 6000
Rockville, MD 20849-6000
United States
Phone: 301-519-5500
Toll-Free: 800-851-3420
TTY: 877-712-9279
Fax: 301-519-5212
http://www.ncjrs.org/

National Institute on Drug Abuse: Club Drugs
6001 Executive Boulevard
Bethesda, MD 20892-9561
United States
Phone: 301-443-1124
Fax: 301-443-7397
http://www.clubdrugs.org/

Office for Victims of Crime (OVC)
810 7th Street, NW
US Department of Justice
Washington, DC 20531
United States
Phone: 202-307-5983
Toll-Free: 800-627-6872
Fax: 202-514-6383
http://www.ojp.usdoj.gov/ovc

Office of Juvenile Justice and Delinquency Prevention (OJJDP)
810 7th Street, NW
Washington, DC 20531
United States
Phone: 202-307-5911
Toll-Free: 800-638-8736
Fax: 202-307-2093
http://www.ojjdp.ncjrs.org/

Office of Minority Health Resource Center (OMHRC)
PO Box 37337
Washington, DC 20013
United States
Phone: 800-444-6472
TTY: 301-230-7199
Fax: 301-230-7198
http://minorityhealth.hhs.gov/

Office on Violence Against Women (OVW)
145 N Street NE, 10th Floor
Washington, DC 20530
United States
TTY: 202-307-2277
http://www.ovw.usdoj.gov

REFERENCES

American Psychiatric Association (2013). Acute Stress Disorder. *Diagnostic and statistical manual of mental disorders* (5th ed.). Washington, DC: Author.

American Psychiatric Association (2013). Post-Traumatic Stress Disorder. *Diagnostic and statistical manual of mental disorders* (5th ed.). Washington, DC: Author.

Astin, M. C., K. J. Lawrence, and D. W. Foy (1993). "Post-traumatic Stress Disorder among Battered Women: Risk and Resiliency Factors." *Violence and Victims 8*, 17 28.

Brown, Theodore M., and Elizabeth Fee (2002). "Walter Bradford Cannon, Pioneer Physiologist of Human Emotions." *Am J Public Health 92*(10), 1594–1595.

Cascardi, M., K. D. O'Leary, E. E. Lawerence, and K. A. Schlee. (1995). Characteristics of women physically assaulted by their spouses and who seek treatment regarding marital conflict. *Journal of Consulting and Clinical Psychology 63*, 616-623.

Child Welfare Information Gateway. "Professionals Required to Report." Last modified 2015. http://wwwchildwelfare.gov

Department of Justice. "Definition of Domestic Violence." Last modified 2017. https://www.justice.gov/ovw/domestic-violence

Domestic Abuse Intervention Project. "Power and Control Wheel." Accessed 2017. www.duluthmodel.org.

Domestic Abuse Intervention Project. "Cycle of Violence." Accessed 2017. www.duluthmodel.org

"Fantasy." In *Merriam-Webster OnLine.* Accessed 2017. http://www.merriam-webster.com/dictionary/fantasy.

"Hope." In *Merriam-Webster OnLine.* Accessed 2017. http://www.merriam-webster.com/dictionary/hope.

Lawson, D. (2005). "Incidence, Explanations, and Treatment of Partner Violence." *Journal of Counseling and Development 81*, 1.

National Coalition Against Domestic Violence. "Definition of the Cycle of Violence." Accessed 2017. www.ncadv.org.

National Coalition Against Domestic Violence. "Definition of Domestic Violence." Accessed 2017. http://ncadv.org/learn-more/what-is-domestic-violence

Substance Abuse and Mental Health Agency(SAMHSA) Trauma and Justice Strategic Initiative (2014). SAMHSA's Concept of Trauma and Guidance for a Trauma-Informed Approach Accessed 2017 https://store.samhsa.gov/shin/content//SMA14-4884/SMA14-4884.pdf

State of Florida Legislature. Section 741.28(2), Florida Statutes (2017). Accessed 2017. http://www.leg.state.fl.us/statutes/index.cfm?App_mode=Display_Statute&URL=0700-0799/0741/Sections/0741.28.html.

"Trauma." In *Merriam-Webster OnLine.* Accessed 2017. http://www.merriam-webster.com/dictionary/trauma

"Walter Cannon Originates Fight or Flight Theory." *American Journal of Public Health.* Last modified 2017. ncbi.nim.gov.

ABOUT THE AUTHOR

D r. Laura Streyffeler is a licensed mental health counselor, a board certified expert in traumatic stress, and a diplomat of the American Academy of Experts in Traumatic Stress. She is listed in the National Registry of the American Academy of Experts in Traumatic Stress. She is a member of the Premier Speakers Bureau for the National Center for Crisis Management. In addition, she is a credentialed expert in domestic violence and forensic counseling by the American Academy of Forensic Counselors. Dr. Laura maintains a private counseling practice in Fort Myers, Florida, where she provides counseling, expert witness/consulting services, and professional trainings.

CPSIA information can be obtained
at www.ICGtesting.com
Printed in the USA
LVHW04*1428020718
582501LV00005B/30/P